The
Sojourner's
Passport

A BLACK WOMAN'S GUIDE TO HAVING THE LIFE AND LOVE YOU DESERVE

The Sojourner's Passport

Outskirts Press, Inc.
Denver, Colorado

Khadija Nassif

Outskirts Press, Inc.
http://www.outskirtspress.com

ISBN: 978-1-4327-5189-0

Outskirts Press and the "OP" logo are trademarks belonging to Outskirts Press, Inc.

PRINTED IN THE UNITED STATES OF AMERICA

To my mother, Janice H.,
who has been my first and best teacher;

my best friend, Bernadette K. and her daughter Kristina,
who have been constant sources of encouragement;

and my hairstylist, salon owner Cheryl K.,
who has been my business heroine without even knowing it.

Table of Contents

PART I: THE SOJOURNER'S PASSPORT REVEALED

CHAPTER 1

THE SOJOURNER'S PATH: BLACK WOMEN, TAKE BACK YOUR CROWNS

Over the past couple of years I've gradually transitioned into being a sojourner. A sojourner is an African-American woman who exercises full freedom of movement in her life. Being a sojourner isn't about any particular political ideology or religious creed. Freedom of movement is what defines the sojourner. This freedom of movement is coupled with a commitment to keeping the sojourner's path open and available for other African-American women and girls.

A sojourner is free to go wherever she chooses. She is free to leave whenever she wants. She is not confined or trapped—either by other people, or by a prison of her own making.

A sojourner is free to seek self-actualization and follow her bliss wherever it leads her. The way of the sojourner has absolutely no room for groupthink or uniformity. The only constants are: (1) freedom of movement, and (2) a commitment to keeping the path open. The sojourner's path is unique for every woman who chooses to walk it. She makes the path her own. Her travels are her own.

A sojourner is not a refugee. She travels wherever she pleases as a self-respecting Black woman who respects her own unique ethnic history. In fact, she chose the descriptive title "sojourner" in honor of her African-American ancestor, Sojourner Truth. A sojourner is not a beggar. She knows that she brings great value to any place that she visits and any endeavor she chooses to participate in.

A sojourner is not defined by her interactions—if she chooses to have any—with Black men. A sojourner is not emotionally enmeshed with Black men. She can choose to involve herself with Black men who have proven themselves to be of value. She is also free to decline any involvement whatsoever with Black men. Even though she can be angered by the injustice of many Black men's ongoing betrayals and attacks on Black women and children, the sojourner is not emotionally enmeshed in all of that. The sojourner has developed a more clinical detachment from Black men and their many failures and betrayals.

A sojourner does not find her identity in hardship and struggle. There are always challenges in life. But a sojourner does not define herself by them. She does not struggle for the sake of struggling.

How *Big Mama's House* Turned into a Dangerous Prison for Black Women

There's a scene in the movie *The Shawshank Redemption* where a prisoner played by Morgan Freeman explains the concept of an "institutional man" to a new inmate. The Freeman character describes the process in which a prisoner adapts so completely to prison that he can't function on the outside as a free man. Things get to the point where all meaning and ability to function is only found within the confines of the prison walls. This is comparable to the experience of those of us who were raised in all-Black settings. Often, Black folks raised in multicultural environments just don't understand it. It's about more than simply being narrow-minded.

Once upon a time, staying within the Black community socially was a means of protection from a genuinely hostile, physically dangerous, and racist outer community. We're so quick to forget the Black teenagers who were beaten and killed when they strayed into non-Black neighborhoods. These put-you-in-a-hospital-bed beatings frequently happened when I was a teenager in Chicago, in neighborhoods with names like "Marquette Park" and "Cicero."

I remember. Chicago was not unique. It wasn't just White kids who might stomp you to death if you came around them. The Mexicans were also good for that sort of thing. In the Chicago context, racist Whites would often unite with racist Latinos against Blacks. These racist White neighborhoods allowed Latinos to move in. Many of our parents told us to stick with "our own" socially—literally to save our lives. They weren't trying to harm or unnecessarily limit us. So, let's not forget that not-insignificant detail.

Another reason many of our parents encouraged us to stick with our own is because they grew up in an era where all of one's social needs could be met within a Black environment. In my mother's day (and earlier), any Black woman who wanted a husband was reasonably assured of being able to find one within Black circles. Many of our parents never anticipated a day when the dangers and pitfalls of remaining within all-Black settings would outweigh the dangers and pitfalls of mingling with the wider society.

Also, the denial and delusions of some early Black extreme multiculturalists horrified many of us raised in all-Black settings. We saw that for many of these people, paradise was with anything and anyone non-Black. We also noticed that they hated all things Black. They mostly pretended that anti-Black racism didn't exist, and then were often blindsided and shocked (*shocked, I say!*) when they were victimized by an agent of racism.

There are other options between these two extremes. It is possible to sojourn in other environments while maintaining one's ethnic and racial self-respect. It is possible to be a sojourner.

Times and circumstances have changed. Behavior patterns that used to be adaptive are now maladaptive to current circumstances. What was originally intended to be protective has atrophied into a prison.

The so-called Black community has become so violent and dysfunctional that it is physically safer for a Black woman to be outside it, rather than inside. The Black family has disintegrated to the point that the odds are against a Black woman finding a husband from within the so-called Black community. And yet, Black women are still being socialized to stay within the confines of Black social circles.

Because of continued residential segregation, all-Black settings are all that some of us know. We work with others, but then we return to our all-Black, segregated areas. However, if Black women want to have fulfilling lives, we'll have to venture outside our all-Black comfort zones. We'll have to leave the prison yard.

Increasing numbers of African-American women are divesting from the nonreciprocal, exploitative interactions that prevail in all-Black social constructs. Every sojourner has divested from such things, but not every woman who divests is a sojourner. Many Black women have escaped the prison of Black residential areas and all-Black social constructs, but are still not sojourners. Let's discuss in some detail what a sojourner is *not*.

A Sojourner Is Not an Institutionalized Prisoner (IP)

A sojourner is not an institutionalized prisoner (IP). An IP can't even imagine life outside the prison yard. IPs are deeply afraid of the outside because they feel there is no place for them there. And so they choose to remain imprisoned.

I've realized that it's not that African-American women are oh-so pro-Black; they simply feel that they have no other places to go. It's not that African-American women just love Black men that much; they simply have the erroneous belief that they have no other options.

African-American women have been deceived. This mass deception has them believing that they must remain in all-Black social constructs. This is consistent with the observations I made during the two previous decades that I spent as a Black Nationalist. From what I've seen, African-Americans of both genders are generally pro-Black in lip service only.

Some IPs can't function on the outside in their current state. They would have to make extensive internal and external changes to navigate the outside world. This includes changes in thought, behavior, and external self-presentation. Many IPs don't want to change anything that they're doing. All of this leads to IPs demanding that other Black women remain imprisoned, so that prison life can remain bearable for the IPs. Misery loves company.

A Sojourner Is Not a Resentful Prisoner

Resentful prisoners (RPs) can imagine and see examples of life on the outside. Some RPs can remember what things were like before the prison. Some RPs remember when what has now become a prison was still Big Mama's House. RPs are usually focused on trying to: (1) convert the prison back into Big Mama's House, or (2) escape into a good, decent, married life that Elijah Muhammad described as "money, good homes, and friendship in all walks of life."

The core problem with the first mission is that it's impossible. We can't ever go back to how it was at Big Mama's House. Big Mama's House was the result of a specific set of historical circumstances. Circumstances have changed, and African-Americans don't have the collective will to rebuild Big Mama's House. That leaves escape as the only viable option.

The core problem with the RPs' escape plans is that they all depend on Black men's cooperation. That endlessly hoped for cooperation from Black men is not forthcoming. RPs are deeply angered by the massive, ongoing betrayals of the Black men who escaped. RPs discovered that Black men lied when they said they were going to help reconstruct Big Mama's House. They lied when they said they would take Black women and children with them when they escaped.

Instead, Black men sought their own individual bliss and left Black women and children behind in Black residential hellholes. The Black men that left generally escape into lives of endless sexual conquests without marriage, illegitimate children that they never live with, and minimal weekend and telephone parenting. Or these men escape into lives of offering "money and good homes" to non-Black women.

RPs refuse to move on from this point. Instead of making their own escape plans, RPs stand around the prison yard (justifiably) berating the escaped Black males who betrayed them. I was a resentful prisoner for many years. Then I escaped.

A Sojourner Is Not Simply an Escaped Prisoner (EP)

Escaped prisoners (EPs) live on the outside. They're often disoriented by being outside the prison. This is because the only identities and self-definitions that many EPs are familiar with are within the prison walls. Many EPs are unsure of where to go or what to do. For them, prison routines don't apply to life on the outside. Some EPs are still caught up in the impossible mission of rebuilding Big Mama's House.

Like the RPs, many EPs are preoccupied with the false promises that Black men made to Black women and children—and they're angry about them. Many EPs refuse to move on emotionally from this point. Healthier EPs have developed a more clinical detachment from Black men and their many failures and betrayals. I transitioned from being a resentful prisoner into being a disoriented, escaped prisoner.

A Sojourner Is Not a Refugee

A sojourner is not a refugee. Refugees learn new routines and ways of living on the outside. But they do so as servile beggars to non-Black people. Refugees have absolutely no ethnic or racial self-respect. Instead of traveling among outsiders as self-respecting people with their own proud history, refugees seek to lose themselves among outsiders.

Like others, some refugees are still emotionally enmeshed with Black men's ongoing betrayals and failures regarding Black women and children. As a result, these enraged refugees will eagerly support any and all tongue-lashings of Black men—even when they come from racists. Other refugees have developed a more clinical detachment.

A Sojourner Is More than Just an Escaped Prisoner

A sojourner is more than just an escaped prisoner. She is committed to keeping the sojourner's path open and available for other African-American women and girls. This commitment includes spreading the good news about the path. It also involves opposing anybody who does anything that blocks Black women's access to becoming a sojourner. A sojourner helps to keep the path open while still seeking her own bliss. The way of the sojourner does not include exchanging one form of martyrdom for another.

I gradually transitioned into walking the sojourner's path. Each sojourner has her own path to follow. I praise God that I made it onto this path. I hope you'll also claim your passport and take up the sojourner's path.

Black Women, Take Back Your Crowns

My sisters, you were robbed of your birthright. Look around. In this country, no other group of women is living like the majority of African-American women. You already know the details. You know the statistics that show the absence of marriage among us. You know the overwhelming majority of our children are born out of wedlock. You know the generations of chaos and suffering that these conditions create.

You also know that other women generally aren't living like this. You know that other women in this country enjoy having reasonable opportunities for legitimate, wholesome marriages and family life. You know that women from other races in this country enjoy having reasonable opportunities to have their beauty and value recognized. They enjoy reasonable opportunities to have fulfilling lives that they love. These benefits are the feminine crowns that these other women are proudly wearing.

My sisters, you also deserve to enjoy these benefits. You also deserve to wear crowns. It is your birthright as women to have reasonable opportunities for legitimate, wholesome marriages and family life—just like it is for every other woman. It is your birthright as women to have your beauty and value recognized. It is your birthright to have reasonable opportunities for fulfilling lives that you love.

However, your crowns were stolen from you. You've been robbed of your birthright by artificially narrowed options and circumstances. These circumstances are the result of African-American women buying into corrupt dogma. Because of them, African-American women are settling for far less than what they are rightfully due.

Most of these dogmas encourage African-American women to accept and normalize conditions that are totally abnormal. There's nothing normal about almost an entire race of women living alone, raising children alone, and dying alone. There's nothing normal about a group of women being expected to socialize young boys into manhood. This sort of lifestyle for a group of women is unheard of in the annals of human history. I suspect the reason is because it doesn't work. Instead, this lifestyle ultimately destroys the women (and the group) who attempt to live like this. The women ultimately collapse from mental, emotional, and physical exhaustion. Large numbers of African-American women are collapsing from all sorts of ailments such as high blood pressure and diabetes. The group ultimately destroys itself in a maelstrom of chaos. That's what's happening in Black residential areas, which are imploding from increasing waves of violence and crime.

Regarding working African-American women, I challenge anyone to tell me exactly how our collective quality of life is substantially different from that of our enslaved foremothers. For most of us, there is never enough of what we need, let alone any abundance in our lives. For most of us, there are no men to protect or provide for us and our children. For most of us, there is no true fellowship. Instead, there is plenty of misery that loves company.

There's no need for you to feel embarrassed or ashamed of your missing crown. There's no shame in being robbed—and you *were* robbed. There's also no need to blame yourself. Most people accept, without questioning, whatever is considered "normal" in their immediate circles. There are also many people who benefit from your stolen crown. These people have a high investment in discouraging you from questioning the absence of your stolen crown.

You Can Take Back Your Crown

What if you found out there is a way to take back your crown and have a life that you love? Would the knowledge of this possibility change the way you live the rest of your life? Would you reach out to claim your crown?

I know that many of you are exhausted. Sometimes, there's a

communication gap between those who are preaching uplift to African-American women and many audience members. Many of the "preachers" have never experienced the complete and utter exhaustion that some audience members are living with.

I know. I understand. I've felt the same way in the past. In the past, I've felt as if I just couldn't contemplate doing anything more or anything different. I do understand, but if you want your crown, you will have to press on. Help is *not* on the way for African-American women. If you don't keep moving forward, even with small steps, you won't make it. It's that simple.

The Sojourner's Passport to an Abundant Life

There is a way for African-American women to have fulfilling lives. There is a passport to abundance for African-American women: *The Sojourner's Passport.* The sojourner philosophy and passport to abundant life are the result of a series of essays and conversations at my blog, *Muslim Bushido.* The sojourner passport to abundant life requires several key steps:

Acknowledging and Speaking the Truth. Many of the problems that are destroying African-American women, as well as the African-American collective, are the result of our mass refusal to acknowledge or speak the truth. We've replaced the truth with obsolete slogans and a totally dishonest discourse. If you want to claim your passport into a better life, you have to be willing to acknowledge and speak the truth.

The most important point to understand is that most life-damaging problems facing African-American women stem from a lack of reciprocity. African-American women suffer because they invest most of their time and energy into people, places, and things that can't and won't give reciprocal support. Women from other groups generally get something of value (be it tangible or intangible in the form of emotional support) in return for their support. Any African-American woman who wants a better life will have to learn how to withdraw from people, places, and things that don't offer a reasonable return on her investment.

Unlike many of the books that claim to address African-American issues while simultaneously walking on eggshells, you'll find that the essays and conversations in *The Sojourner's Passport* speak the plain truth.

Critical Thinking. If you want to claim your passport for a better life, you have to be willing to engage in critical thinking. *The Sojourner's Passport* will challenge you to take a fresh look at the people, places, and things in which you invest your time and energy.

Leaving the Hive Mentality Behind. Many African-American women are trapped in a hive mentality that says, "I shouldn't or can't make any moves toward an abundant life until there's a solution in place for every single African-American in this country." There are several flaws with this notion.

First, there won't be any solution for the masses of African-Americans. They are well on their way to forming a permanent underclass in this country. The lifestyle choices and modern cultural norms underlying permanent underclass status (out-of-wedlock births, single parenting, a lack of respect for education, a refusal to set or adhere to any standards) are too far gone to be reversed.

Finally, Black women are the only ones narrowing their life options out of a misguided sense of racial loyalty. In contrast, Black men consistently exercise their right to seek their own bliss. Black men consistently do whatever works best for them, with or without Black women.

If you want to claim your passport into a better life, you have to be willing to leave the hive mentality behind. *The Sojourner's Passport* will challenge you to reexamine the hive mentality and many other unspoken assumptions underlying your previous choices.

Stepping Outside Your Comfort Zones. If you want to claim your passport into a better life, you have to be willing to step out-side your comfort zones. Reclaiming your crown means taking your rightful place on the global stage and within the global village. It's impossible for an African-American woman to do this while remaining locked within increasingly spirit-crushing, soul-killing, and life-damaging all-Black social and residential enclaves. *The Sojourner's Passport* will challenge you to step out of these famil-iar but harmful spaces and enter the global village.

CHAPTER 2

MY DARK-SKINNED SISTERS, STOP LETTING BIRACIAL, BICULTURAL, MULTICULTURAL, AND LIGHT-SKINNED WOMEN WEAR YOUR STOLEN CROWNS

My Sisters, Let's Be Clear about Your Stolen Crowns

Black men stole your crown. In earlier decades, Black men stole your crown of recognized beauty and gave it to light-skinned women like me. I've watched and denounced this practice since I was in high school in the early 1980s. I hate oppression. Which is why I've always rejected stolen goods. Especially stolen goods based on devaluing Blackness. I've always rejected Black men who have a fetish for light skin. You see, my crown does not depend on devaluing other women. My crown rests on my head because it belongs there, based on my own individual charms. I don't want a crown stolen from some other woman.

Dominance through Hair Flips

Unlike some of the other light-skinned girls in my high school,

I didn't prance down the hallways while making sure to flip my hair in the presence of darker-skinned girls. We know what the hair flip was all about. It's an act of dominance by Black women who have so-called "good hair." It's intended to put those without so-called good hair in their assigned place. Which is somewhere beneath the woman who is doing the hair flip.

First, my hair (even while permed) does not flip. Second, despite other people's eager suggestions, I was never interested in pursuing concoctions (gel, carefree curls) that might have given my hair a more flippable appearance. Most importantly, I came to hate the entire scenario. So, I had my hair cut into a natural. Of course, other Black people were horrified. The common refrain from other Blacks was, "You let somebody cut off your hair? You need to find the person who did that, and get your money back!"

Let's be real. I had the self-confidence to do this as a teenager because I was light-skinned. I knew (in the back of my mind) that no matter what I did, my light skin would ensure that I got some favorable attention from Black males.

I know how painful it is to talk about this. I know that talking about this is pulling at half-healed scabs. But we need to be able to talk honestly about these things. As Black women, we need to get our crowns back, and take our rightful place on the global stage. I was going to do a post about Black consciousness. Then I realized that nothing (including consciousness of any sort) is possible without a foundation of self-determination. Self-determination means that we think, speak, and define things for ourselves. It means looking at the world through our own eyes. And we can't have self-determination when we cooperate with other people assigning lower value to us. Collectively, we've got to get our crowns back. To recover our crowns, we need to understand how they were taken away. And how we sometimes unintentionally cooperate with this mass theft.

Many Black Women's Bad Faith and Collaboration with Oppression

I've raised my voice against intra-Black colorism since high school. Over the years, I've had very few light-skinned sisters in arms speaking out against this with me. Most of us didn't have our darker sisters' backs back in the day. Many light-skinned Black women did not take Black men's self-hating choices seriously until these choices began to put a crimp in *their* lives—until they lost their spot at the top of the preferred-by-Black-men heap. Until Negroes snatched the already-stolen-from-darker-sisters crowns off *their* heads, and placed them on the heads of Becky, Lupe, J. Lo, and Mei Ling.

This is an example of bad faith, not any solidarity. From what I hear, it hasn't gone unnoticed by darker sisters.

However, I've also noticed that many darker sisters cooperate with the robbery, aiding and abetting those stealing their crowns. Often, we have allowed Black male thieves to redefine the theft of our crowns as a matter of their "personal preferences." Let me give some examples:

When a Black male celebrity such as Ne-Yo says, "All the prettiest kids are light-skinned anyway," he's stealing your crown, and giving it to light-skinned women. If you persist in listening to, and buying this creature's products, you are helping him snatch your crown off your head and put it on somebody else's head.

When a Black male celebrity such as Yung Berg says that he doesn't date "dark butts," he's stealing your crown. If you persist in listening to, and buying this creature's products, you are helping him steal your crown.

These are obvious examples of collaboration. There are many that are less obvious. When you embrace mediocrity in your self-presentation, you are helping to validate Black men stealing your crown. You are also helping to validate other women's decision to wear your stolen crown.

Verbal Hair Flips and Collaboration through Inappropriate Inclusion

Unfortunately, some of us have grown so accustomed to being assigned a lower value, that we accept this as normal. There are verbal hair flips that many of us accept, and don't even recognize as dominance and aggression. We feel their effects, but we don't make the connection between the verbal hair flips and our battered spirits.

One verbal hair flip is when a woman makes sure that you know she's so-called biracial, bicultural, or multicultural. There are normal, self-respecting Black people who happen to have one parent who isn't Black. Or they have one parent who is Black, but is not African-American. At some later point when it comes up naturally (such as when you meet their parents), you find out the person has a non-Black or non-African-American parent. Such a person's identity and claim to fame does not revolve around making a distinction between themselves and Black or African-American people. These are people who are acting in good faith by rejecting stolen goods—stolen goods that rest on devaluing Blackness or African-Americans.

This is quite different from self-proclaimed biracial, bicultural, or multicultural persons who want to make sure that you know that they are *not* Black like you. From so-called mulattoes within ancient African societies to apartheid-era South African "Colored," to the "biracials" here and now among us, these "I don't want to be Black, and Whites won't let me be White" people have done great harm to Black people's interests.

Throughout our history, Black people have allowed these "biracial" types to form a wedge, and a disloyal fifth column among the Black collective. Where do you think the Black-skinned, yet self-proclaimed "Arabs" in Darfur came from? They came from partially Arab, so-called biracial, and bicultural people. Where do you think the mostly collaborating Coloreds in apartheid-era

South Africa came from? Throughout our people's history, what these internal enemies all have in common is their obsession with being recognized as something other than, and distinct from, Black.

Another observed pattern with self-proclaimed biracials is that they want to be considered Black like any other Black person when there's something to be gained, such as scholarships from Black organizations and affirmative action slots. When there's nothing to be gained and nothing to be stolen from Black people, then they want you to know how distinct they are from Black people.

We need to stop cooperating with this theft of our resources. If so-called biracial, bicultural, and multicultural people want to be distinct from Blacks, then we need to require them to be distinct all the way. Cut them off from Black folks' scholarships, set-asides and other resources. Make them find biracial scholarships for biracial people. Stop helping them steal from Black people's meager resources. Stop including these people.

In the crown context, stop celebrating these self-proclaimed biracial, multicultural, and bicultural women wearing your stolen crown! Stop lifting them up. Stop claiming them as part of our collective. Stop worrying about them. Purge them and their problems from your list of concerns. These women don't need your help. They have plenty of worshipful Black male slaves (like Ne-Yo, Yung Berg, many in the NFL, and others) to attend to their needs. Don't fall for the lie that says, "They're part of us." Didn't these self-proclaimed biracial, bicultural, and multicultural people already tell you that they are something *other than* part of us? That they are *anything but Black*? Why are some of you so eager to claim them when they are not claiming you? Especially when they are wearing your stolen crown?

Celebrate Yourself and the Women Most Like You First

We're going to need some affirmative action among ourselves to get this situation righted. I mean affirmative action regarding whom we hold up to our children (and ourselves) as representing our ideal "look." The "color neutral" and "let's celebrate our internal rainbow" doesn't work because of everything that has come before it. It's similar to Whites wanting to play color-blind after centuries of accumulated injustice went down. In both examples, doing this leaves preexisting problems firmly in place.

As Black women, we have the power to turn this around. How? By taking back our crowns and taking our rightful place on the global stage. It doesn't matter what most Black men think about us. Since most of them don't protect or provide for us, they are generally of no or low value to us. The only thing that matters is what we think about ourselves.

Ladies, if you have Black-oriented magazines in your homes, whose images are you surrounding yourselves (and your children, if you have any) with? Are you surrounding yourself with images of White women's children like Alicia Keys? Halle Berry? Lisa Bonet? Persia White? Rashida Jones? Jennifer Beals? Jasmine Guy? Victoria Rowell? Are you surrounding yourself with images of Black women who look like White women's children like Vanessa Williams? Are you watching music videos packed with biracial, light-skinned women? If so, have you considered the possibility that this is not healthy for your psyche?

If all the above is true, are you willing to find images that affirm you and women who look more like you?

Black self-hatred is so deeply entrenched that it will be a long, long time before people like me are in any real danger of having our self-worth assaulted because of corrective internal affirmative action . I don't feel threatened by efforts to raise my darker sisters up so their beauty can also be appreciated. Everyone has her own rightful crown. Collectively, we need to get ours back. Nobody is going to voluntarily return our stolen crowns to us. A thief never returns what he has taken. We're going to have to snatch our crowns back ourselves. The first step is to stop aiding and abetting the thieves.

CHAPTER 3

BLACK WOMEN, ARE YOU READY TO FEEL FLAWLESS?

About Catherine Deneuve

Catherine Deneuve first came to my attention when I was in college. My boyfriend wanted to see the movie *The Hunger*. Like some guys, he was excited about the idea of seeing some on-screen lesbian action. I later returned the favor by letting him watch me avidly stare at Steven Bauer throughout *Thief of Hearts*. At any rate, while I sat through *The Hunger* I was fascinated by Ms. Deneuve's clothes and how she carried herself. I've never been particularly jealous of other women's gifts. I was simply amazed that a middle-aged woman could look so good—especially a White woman, because they usually don't age very well. Even many half-White women don't age well. (Exhibit No. 1: Jasmine Guy. What in the world happened? Why does her skin look so— leathery?) Oops. Maybe I should have given the preamble that I'm going to speak candidly here. I feel the self-worth issues underlying this topic are too important for me to walk on eggshells, so be prepared to be offended (in parts).

Well, right then and there, I decided that I wanted to look like Catherine Deneuve when I was middle-aged. She looked fabulous without looking trashy, tacky, or trying to dress like a twenty-year-old. This is what I found off-putting (at times) about Tina Turner or Patti LaBelle. There was also the negative example of a middle-aged White woman on campus who liked to pick up and sleep with college boys. This woman wore the same Esprit dresses that many of the college girls were wearing at the time. It was not a good look for her, although, I guess it served her purpose. Some young men even made up a chant about her with the chorus, "I'm not sleepin' alone!"

Anyway, decades have passed since college. I'm now middle-aged like Catherine Deneuve was when she starred in *The Hunger*. After having forgotten about her for years, Catherine Deneuve came back to mind one day recently. And I realized that I do not look together like Catherine Deneuve! Meanwhile, Catherine Deneuve has still kept herself together as a senior citizen. No wonder she has remained a cultural icon in her native France *for over forty years!*

What went wrong? Several interlocking things that affect far too many Black women. First, I never took the time to develop a signature look. I have clothes that look good in isolation. But, there's no overall look that I've established for myself. This is not good. Second, at some point, like so many Black women, I got into the habit of settling for looking good enough. One of my college friends had an amazing spirit. Whenever somebody asked her how she felt, more often than not, she would say, "Flawless." Unfortunately, even though I admired her spirit, I never really bought into the "flawless" state of mind. Until now. Until I decided that next spring is the deadline to get a new wardrobe and have myself together like Catherine Deneuve. So, I'm doing a lot of fashion research right now.

I've been thinking about this a lot recently because it intersects with so many issues that confront most Black women: self-worth issues, cultural issues, and class issues. Too often, we call certain attitudes "modesty" when they really reflect a lack of self-worth.

Let me be clear: I am not talking about using clothes (or other material things) as magic totems to acquire self-respect or status. I am talking about how many Black women's exteriors reflect a total lack of self-worth. In the milder version of this phenomenon, most Black women's exteriors don't come anywhere near the level of their internal selves.

Settling for Looking Sort-of Good Enough

I was blessed to grow up with a dad who told me that I was "the prettiest, smartest, and *best* little girl in the world." My father has a superiority complex. I believe that it's justified in his case. He *really does* have many gifts that are superior to those of most others that I've observed. Looking at him as an adult, I can see that he's an extremely smart, aggressive, and shrewd alpha male. Of course, his praise of me has always been partially a reflection of his own ego. That's fine. Whatever works. My parents' constant positive reinforcement spared me from having the insecurities about my looks that plague most Black women. Of course, my light skin enhances my perceived looks among most Black people.

But, above and beyond Black folks' color issues, I always felt a base of self-confidence in the looks department because of my dad, even when his praise was tempered by my own observations as a teenager and young woman. I realized then that, no, I wasn't the prettiest. But I was content in feeling "pretty enough." I felt pretty enough to attract the attention of a reasonable number of men. I didn't buy into feeling "flawless," but I felt pretty enough to hold my head high. Pretty enough was my baseline.

Unfortunately, most African-American women did not have a father like mine. They didn't grow up with a circle of adult male relatives constantly telling them that they were beautiful. From what I can tell from conversations I've had over the years, most Black women don't feel pretty enough. Most of us don't even feel pretty. The mass baseline for our self-perception in the looks department hovers somewhere between "I'm ugly, but just maybe I can get by" to "I sort of look good enough."

Settling for looking "sort of good enough" is manifested in so many ways. You can see it in our not taking care of our bodies, allowing ourselves to become visibly overweight, or by failing to develop a polished look.

By the way, gentlemen, much of this discussion also applies to you. Don't feel left out of the observation simply because I'm focusing on the women. Sirs, please conduct the following spot check on yourselves: Stand nude in front of a full-length mirror. This is usually a *revelation* for most people. I'm often reminded of how my (straight) Southern Black man colleague muttered under his breath when looking at another Black male attorney in court. The gentleman was wearing a too-tight double-breasted suit that did not flatter (or conceal) his potbelly. My coworker muttered, "Too much damn sausage."

I've also been taken aback by how so many Sunni ("orthodox") Muslim Black women choose grim and drab fabrics and colors for their hijabs. Judging from the behaviors and reactions I've observed at some mosques, I suspect that many Muslim Black women especially like hijab because it gives them an opportunity to hide. It gives them a chance to opt out of caring about their looks. Essentially, they choose to lose gracefully when compared with other women.

Ultimately, few Black women truly feel that they can hold their own in the looks department. So, it's no surprise that few Black women feel entitled to feel "flawless."

Cultural Issues: Americans and Others Are Slovenly Compared with the French

I noticed this when traveling in Europe a couple of years ago. You could almost always pick out the American tourists from others. Overweight. Blue jeans. Tennis shoes. It's almost like a uniform. It reminded me of the slum uniform for young Black men. Long white T-shirts (that to me, almost look like T-shirt dresses). Sagging jeans. Tennis shoes. As far as I'm concerned, these uniforms are not an attractive look. They don't reflect self-respect. I also noticed that the French generally don't look like this.

These different cultural attitudes toward one's appearance come up in a memoir called *Almost French* by Sarah Turnbull. It's an account by an Australian woman who moves to France with her French boyfriend. One Saturday morning, she decides to wear sweatpants to go to the neighborhood bakery for baguettes. He was horrified. She describes how their different cultural attitudes about self-presentation were a long-term source of tension in their relationship. She mentions that the French have an expression, *se mettre en valeur*. It means to make the most of yourself. This is expected in France.

I believe the French view is correct. Self-maintenance is a mark of self-respect, and one that is sorely lacking among many African-Americans. It's also important to note that the French approach to personal appearance takes self-discipline.

Class Matters: Elite Women Are Trained to Have Themselves Together in All Sorts of Ways

Every arena in life has its own rules. Too often, Black folks like to pretend that these rules don't exist or that they don't matter. The rules always matter. It would be more honest for us to say that: (1) we will avoid entering certain arenas because we don't know, and are not willing to learn, the rules; or (2) we are willing to act in ways that are inappropriate to the arena because we refuse to learn or honor the rules.

When I encountered Black elite girls or young women in high school or college, I could tell that they had been coached in certain ways. I never took the time to investigate the world of finishing schools or debutante balls, but I knew these things existed. I also knew there were rules to these things, and that I had no clue about them. I didn't grow up being taken to black-tie events by my parents. Because I didn't grow up going to formal social events, I never learned certain details like the correct way of handing off my coat to the butler, or the right technique to get in and out of a limo. Let's not even get into all the intricate table manners surrounding five-course formal meals that I don't know.

There's no shame in not knowing these details if you weren't raised that way. However, that doesn't take away the fact that I'm not polished or poised in this arena. It's the same way Michelle Obama is not polished or poised. She (or her husband's staff) had to hire people to hook her up with this information. I would also have to hire people to learn these things. If somebody has to coach you as an adult in these matters, then you are behind the curve in this particular arena. There's no shame in this fact. It is simply a fact. I don't feel any compelling urge to learn these details. This information is not essential for my lifestyle. However, I am also not going to redefine "polish" and "poise" to accommodate my ignorance of these matters. The bottom line is that elite girls are trained to know all of these things by the time they are teenagers.

Elite girls are also consciously raised to be much more careful about their appearance in general. They might choose to rebel and break the rules, but they know what the rules are. In this way, the old-money rich really *are* different from the rest of us.

- Are you ready to feel flawless? Are you willing to *se mettre en valeur*—to make the most of yourself?
- Are you ready to feel flawless, and make the most of yourself with the body you have right now? Even if you have things to work on with your body (and who doesn't), you don't have to wait to feel flawless. Too many women tell themselves, "Oh, I'll buy a new, flattering wardrobe when

I get down to size _____." I believe that this is a demoralizing mistake.

- Are you willing to commit to the discipline that it takes to truly feel flawless? For example, are you willing to seek out ways to feel flawless with whatever budget you have?
- Are you willing to stop stepping out of the house looking subpar? You can't feel flawless if the public has already seen you looking lousy on so-called "off days."

CHAPTER 4

FIRST, LOVE YOURSELF AS AN AFRICAN-AMERICAN WOMAN

After some reflection, I realized that those of us walking the sojourner's path need to start having some conversations immediately about issues we face along the way. And these are going to have to be difficult, grown-up conversations about some painful and complex things.

Here's why: As African-Americans, we have a history of falling into one calamity after another. When we fail to protect our ethnic self-respect, even our solutions become new, self-destructive problems. I don't want that painful pattern to be repeated with *The Sojourner's Way*. I know our people. I know that many African-American women, just like many African-American men, are looking for the nearest exit out of our African-American identity.

Have you noticed that people who are racially all-Black, but are one-half African-American and one-half another Black ethnicity almost always identify themselves by their non-African-American half? The overall pattern is that whenever there's a choice between identifying as African-American and anything else (including a foreign Black ethnicity), people rarely choose to identify as African-American. Instead, those of us whose physical appearance can justify it start emphasizing our 1/677th Cherokee, Irish, and whatever else is non-Black ancestry. Those of us whose physical appearances don't lend themselves to playing Tiger Woods' "I'm Cablanasian" game start positioning our children to disappear into other people's gene pool.

By contrast, a sojourner walks with sincere and deep pride in her African-American heritage. This is why I'm careful to describe myself and our people as both Black and African-American. It's important to have racial self-respect (which is lacking throughout Africa and the African diaspora). But it's also important for African-Americans to have ethnic self-respect specifically as African-Americans.

From my view, the problem with calling ourselves only "Black" is that this label is not specific to our people as African-Americans. It's not specific to the Black people born in this country, who are descended from those Africans who were held in slavery here. When we only refer to ourselves as Black, we make ourselves a blank slate relative to other Black people who also have specific cultural identities, such as Haitians, Jamaicans, Trinidadians, Nigerians, Panamanians, and others.

By saying only Black, we put ourselves in a culturally weak position relative to these other Black people. This is why many African-Americans often get upset when foreign Blacks come to us with statements such as, "On my island" or, "In my country, we do blah-blah" and so on. Other types of Blacks are quick to tell us about their islands and countries. There's nothing wrong with that. People are supposed to feel good about their heritage.

What do we as African-Americans have to say in response? Usually nothing, because most of us don't take the time to find out things that we can feel equally proud of. That's not other people's fault. It's our own fault when we don't seek to develop our ethnic pride. I don't have a problem with hearing "on my island" statements from foreign Blacks because I have my own family traditions to talk about. When they tell me about their traditions, I start talking happily about what my grandparents always said and believed.

By saying only "Black," we verbally erase our people's entire specific, shared history.

Furthermore, do not interpret any of this as some sort of broadside against any other blogger. As I've said before, we're going to have to start having some more adult conversations. This means exploring different takes on various ideas. Disagreement on one or even more points does not automatically mean disrespect or disparagement of those with other views. As I said in an earlier post, making room for dissenting views is essential to our survival. We must learn to take what is useful from a point of view and discard the rest. Without rancor.

Avoid Becoming a Refugee

As I said earlier, a sojourner is not a refugee. Refugees learn new routines and ways of living on the outside. But they do so as servile beggars to non-Black people. Refugees have no ethnic or racial self-respect. Instead of traveling among outsiders as self-respecting people with their own proud history, refugees seek to lose themselves among outsiders.

Unless we make a conscious decision to find and strengthen our basis for ethnic self-respect as African-Americans, we will inevitably turn into self-hating, Black-hating refugees. This is exactly what our people have done with previous paths such as integration and multiculturalism. Because of not securing our ethnic self-respect, many of us started carrying water for other people (be they non-Blacks, foreign Blacks, or biracials) once we got on these previous paths.

This is also what our people have previously done when we sought to lose ourselves in a purely religious identity. Many African-American Muslims (mostly men) have already fallen into this self-hating, Black-hating trap. Abdur-Rahman Muhammad, blog host of *A Singular Voice*, talked about this in his excellent series, "*Why Blackamerican Muslims Don't Stand for Justice.*" He described many of the disgraceful, self-hating practices that many African-American Sunni Muslim men have adopted. As I explain in Chapter 12, there is a major difference between Sunni Islam and Minister Farrakhan's Nation of Islam. The problems with Black American Muslim self-hatred, and support for terrorism are all coming from the Sunni Black Muslims, and not from the Nation of Islam. I'm saying this as a Sunni Muslimah. I have never been a member of the Nation of Islam.

African-American Sunni Muslim men have adopted practices such as flying to Morocco to buy Arab wives. They do so out of a belief in Arab racial superiority (if it was simply about having a non-Western wife who speaks Arabic, they could seek out Black African Muslim wives). Many of these self-hating Muslim Black men also adopt fake Arab and Pakistani accents, and attempt to pass as non-Black. This is similar to the way that self-hating Black parents of don't-you-dare-call-me-Black biracials desperately want their children to pass into non-Blackness. One example of this is Tiger Woods and his father.

Ethnic self-hatred creates a dilemma. It causes African-Americans to try to flee their ethnic heritage. But the African-American person who tries to run from their African-American heritage makes themselves less likely to be accepted (much less respected) by non-African-Americans. These refugees become a joke, or at best a mascot, to other people.

If you choose to misidentify African-American culture by the modern hip hop crack house dysfunction, isn't it logical for non-African-Americans to define you by that? If you (because of a lack of ethnic pride) agree that African-American heritage is a stigma, isn't it logical for non-African-Americans to stigmatize you and your children for this so-called "taint"? This is The Tiger Woods Dilemma. When his fellow anti-Black golfer chose to insult Mr. Woods, he chose to insult his African-American heritage with references to fried chicken. When crafting his insult, he ignored Mr. Woods' Asian heritage. The White, anti-Black golfer attacked the Black, anti-Black golfer with the heritage that they *both* agreed was a stigma: African-American heritage.

It's similar to what I've read about the experiences of self-hating African-American Muslim males in Arab lands. Apparently, many Arabs frequently call these Black men and their half-Arab children the Arabic word for "slave" to their faces. These anti-Black, Black men tolerate this because they inwardly agree that they are tainted because of their African-American heritage.

Those sojourners who are mothers should keep in mind that non-African-American others will be quick to toss the label "African-American" on their children—no matter what ethnicity these children's fathers are, and no matter what ethnic or racial appearance these children have. It's similar to the dynamic I've heard described by Korean-American acquaintances. They've mentioned that relatives from South Korea who never immigrated to the United States are often resentful of them. They've described how resentful Korean relatives sneeringly label the 100-percent-Korean-ancestry Korean-American as "Americans." The old country relatives don't mean the American label in a good way. There's often jealousy, resentment, and downright hatred involved in these interactions.

Sojourners need to understand that if old-country relatives are inclined to do that with American relatives who have 100-percent old-country ancestry, they should imagine what such people will say to a child who is 50-percent African-American. The choice is yours. You will either give your children reasons to feel good about being referred to as African-American, or you leave your children to hang their heads in shame when other people call them that.

African-Americans Are Not Ethnic 'Blank Slates' Who Were Only Previously United by Superficial Characteristics: We Are a People Among Other Peoples

Beware of denying our African-American ethnic group's standing as a separate people among other peoples. Doing so leads to becoming a refugee. This mistaken idea has been the ruin of African-Americans throughout history. This mistaken idea is why, up to now, most of us have never been able to maintain our ethnic self-respect in the presence of others.

Nature abhors a vacuum. That's why African-Americans' past attempts to become ethnic blank slates by denying our shared history and culture has always led to self-hatred. That's why I'm on high alert on this topic. Be especially cautious of such arguments coming from foreign Blacks who claim the benefits of "peoplehood" for themselves while they deny it to us.

The old slave-breakers had to sever our ancestors' connections to each other by force. In the modern era, people (including those who might mean us well, and never consciously intended to hurt us) sever African-Americans' connections to one another by mistake or by guile. In previous eras, African-Americans were confused enough to go along with having our peoplehood negated by others, but no more.

Don't Tap Dance on Black Unity's Grave: Doing So Leads to Becoming a Refugee

Black Unity has been dead for some time. The aftershocks caused by "his " senility and death are the reasons African-American women must flee most Black residential areas to save our lives and live in safety, as will be discussed in Chapter 6.

Give credit where it is due to Black Unity. I know that many of you are deeply angry at Black Unity, and are therefore eager to dance on his grave. And let's call him a guy, because he *did* favor

Black men's interests over those of Black women and children. This would be unfair *and* a mistake on your part.

Here's why: There's a major distinction to be made between what Black Unity was during his youth and middle age, and what he became during his senility. Black Unity became enfeebled and afflicted with Alzheimer's as he aged. In his senility, he confused the meanings of many of his values. In his senility, he also fathered illegitimate children called The Acting Black Crew.

This is why many of you are justifiably angry at Black Unity. You never got to meet Black Unity in his youth and middle age. Some of you didn't get to grow up in Big Mama's House; you were raised amid a hip hop crack house culture. All you ever saw was a destructive, senile, elderly guy and his illegitimate, ghetto, gangbanger acting-Black offspring.

If you're going to judge Black Unity, judge him by *all* of his actions, not just what he did after he became senile and afflicted with Alzheimer's.

In his youth and middle age, Black Unity was one of Big Mama's best friends and champions. Black Unity protected Big Mama to the best of his ability when nobody else lifted a finger to help her. Among other things he did, Black Unity told African-Americans to stay off those buses after Big Mama Rosa Parks was arrested.

Without Black Unity's efforts, you wouldn't be free enough to travel anywhere. You would do well to remember that.

I love my Big Mama, and I love and praise God Almighty for everybody who ever helped her. Including Black Unity. I don't forgive him his later trespasses. However, I'm still grateful for what he did for me and countless other African-Americans. I give credit where credit is due.

In his youth and middle age, Black Unity kept the worst ravages of African-American self-hatred at bay. We see what happened after he became feeble and senile. We see the escalation of "the paper-bag test" into a "manila folder and lighter test," the near-requirement that Black entertainers be (or look like) White women's children, and flyers at Black events advertising parties for light-skinned women. For all I know, without Black Unity I might have grown up to be the sort of light-skinned Black woman that revels in having light skin, and flipping her hair in the presence of darker-skinned Black women.

In Earlier Eras, We Said Black Unity When We Were Talking about Black Unity within an African-American Context

We've been saying "Black," but what we're actually talking about is a concept (Black Unity) as expressed among African-Americans. The same applies to the concept of The Acting Black Crew.

Because we've been saying "Black" when we're really talking about phenomena that are specific to African-Americans, we allowed foreign Blacks to contribute perspectives that don't necessarily apply to our specific circumstances as African-Americans. This is why sometimes it helps to be specific in identifying the ethnic group one is referencing.

During previous decades, African-Americans also said "Black" when what we were referring to was ourselves in the context of our particular shared history and culture as a separate ethnic group. It took African-Americans centuries to process the evolving idea of how we felt comfortable describing ourselves as a separate ethnic group. But at each stage, African-Americans were referring to ourselves as a separate ethnic group, with our own shared history and culture when we said words like "Colored,"" Negro," "Black," and finally, "African-American."

Do You Have Ethnic Self-Respect as an African-American Woman? If Not, You'll Become a Refugee

What African-Americans historically (and imprecisely) referred to as Black Unity was actually African-American self-love and self-respect. All of which is sorely lacking among African-Americans and Black people in general.

Give credit where it is due to Black Nationalism. From my view, the root of the problem is not primarily with the Black Nationalist ideologies that originally promoted African-American self-love and self-respect. They are more or less as sexist as the rest of the belief systems that African-Americans have adopted over the years. I believe the core problem is with the fundamentalism and groupthink that crept into these ideologies—the same unfortunate evolution that occurs with ideologies and religion in general.

We should, of course, give credit where it is due to Black Nationalism—before he became severely mentally ill. That illness followed years of intense government pressure, including state-sponsored assassinations (such as COINTELPRO). Black Nationalism's mind broke under the pressure, and he became a dangerous, screaming street lunatic.

When most African-Americans were worshipping a historically inaccurate, Aryan image of Jesus, and singing songs begging to be "washed White as snow," Black Nationalism said "no" to that and talked about a Black Messiah.

After racists within the local and federal government originally refused to respond to Dr. King, the later presence of Black Nationalism gave these racists something else to consider. The presence of Black Nationalism encouraged them to make some concessions to the pacifist Civil Rights Movement. In the Cold War context, the presence of a Black Nationalist boogeyman made the integrationist leaders' demands more palatable to racist White politicians.

I'm saying all of this to emphasize that nature abhors a vacuum. You cannot walk the sojourner's path successfully while trying to be an ethnicity-neutral, blank slate. You will become a refugee.

The world is filled with others who have at least some semblance of ethnic self-respect and pride. Whenever "nothing" encounters "something," the "nothing" loses out. If you try to travel among others as a "blank slate," you will lose out.

As sojourners we need to work through the following questions because the answers we find determine the fate of our individual journeys and the path itself.

- Do you feel good about being an African-American woman?

- If not, are you going to look into your family history and our people's collective history to find reasons to feel good about being an African-American woman?

- If we search, we will find something and somebody within our family tree to be proud of. I'm not talking about history-book achievements. I'm talking about the wisdom, perseverance, and courage that our ancestors had. Do you understand there had to have been at least a few individuals within your personal family tree who had these qualities? (If not, then they wouldn't have survived, and you wouldn't be here.)

- Many times, we try to do things the lazy way. The business-as-usual way. Do you understand that the sojourner's path does not work like that?

- Do you understand that hip hop crack house culture is *not* African-American culture?

- If hip hop crack house culture and acting-Black culture are all you know, are you willing to find out who African-Americans were before that madness spread among us?

- Are you willing to walk in dignity with the best of African-American culture?

CHAPTER 5

WHY WE MUST FIRST LOVE OURSELVES AS AFRICAN-AMERICAN WOMEN

While I was blogging, I received this e-mail from a reader and she gave me permission to publish it (I deleted her name and the geographical location of her university) because it might help other young African-American women her age. I agree that it's helpful for others to hear her experiences. Here's her e-mail:

Dear Muslim Bushido, Hello! My name is _____, and I'm a sophomore at a _____ university. I read your latest post, and it really touched me. I feel the need to be honest about this (this is the first time that I'm even saying these things out loud). I'm just now—at 20 years old—learning to accept and love the fact that I'm Black, or African-American.

I'm really embarrassed about this, but there are SOOO many other girls in my position. I'm tired of all of the emotional and mental baggage that comes with not really being who I am. So one day, I just decided to breathe and LET IT GO. I got so sick of mentally tiring myself out with that crap. Reading your blog, along with Evia's and many others, really did awaken something in me. PLEASE believe me when I say that you women are a godsend— I've even told my mother about your blogs, and she STRONGLY

ENCOURAGES me to continue reading.

You see, my strange relationship with all of the foolishness began at an early age—since before I can remember. My father's side of the family is so DEEPLY entrenched in colorism it's scary. My own paternal grandfather divorced my grandmother because his mother did not approve. My father has a disappointing relationship with his mom, to say the least.

My father's many family (without the presence of a male) grew up on welfare, and my father has never forgiven my Granny for that. Any woman that even resembles her on the street is a ' fat black widerbeast'. That's how bad it is. It even goes down to hair. My father was always soo happy that I had long hair, and that I wasn't too dark. His whole side of the family loves to sit around and talk about their mixed heritage—many of my family could pass for Latino. I heard this day in and day out. My mother is a very kind woman, and she is my best friend. But she just puts up with so much foolishness it's ridiculous. I would never want to have the marriage she has with my father.

I have gone through a lot emotionally over the years. I had always wanted to fit in with other groups...I was a refugee. A beggar. I never quite understood why these people did not accept me until now. Through grade school, I even did people's homework and gave them lunch money to keep friends! How pathetic. I remember growing up actually feeling LUCKY that I didn't look all Black. I'd witnessed other girls that did look traditional get teased, and I was glad I was never teased based upon my looks. But I still thought my life would be better if I was lighter with mixed-looking curly hair (I have relaxed hair). I was one of those quasi-mixed looking girls; I was in the middle. I wanted more attention, because I thought I wasn't as pretty as the biracial girls. This thinking is so prevalent it's crazy.

When I went to high school (I went to two), I wanted desperately to be popular. At my first school, the race du jour was Latino. Or if you were a Black girl, you had to be mixed to even be considered. So, many Black girls that could get away with it started lying about their heritage and saying that they were part this or that. I was one of those girls. I have Mexican family members on my father's side of my family (via marriage), so I started telling people my grandfather was Mexican. No one called my bluff, because I had really long hair and spoke excellent Spanish. I was elevated among Blacks, but NOT the Latinos. They still did not accept me. I was a refugee beggar, and they used me, but still didn't befriend me in the end.

So then I moved to another area after my father retired from the military. The previous high school was in a wealthy county with a very diverse student body. This high school was in a poor county that was just developing (although I lived in a prominent neighborhood). This school was mostly comprised of poor Blacks and Whites. I was treated like royalty. I was treated better because I had money, and had long hair. It was also because I was still lying to people about my heritage, only now my grandfather was CUBAN instead of Mexican (it worked better that way, because I could much more easily pass for that).

I even took that lie with me to college. This semester, I decided that I wouldn't tell people that anymore. In the end, nobody really cares what you're mixed with except ignorant Blacks. I soon realized this first semester of my sophomore year. I just got tired—I got tired of the guilt, tired of the low self-esteem, and the hassle of covering up that lie with other lies about my heritage. I'm actually still scared to death that my friends' parents will meet with mine, and that they'll start talking about Cuba or something!

I'm really ready to discover myself AS myself. If you want to post this, I don't mind (it will help others, ESPECIALLY girls my age). Just take my name out! Lol. Thanks.

This is what I said in a response e-mail:

> Don't be embarrassed and don't blame yourself. AA self-disrespect is an airborne contagion. It surrounds most of us

24/7. All of this really should have been straightened out during the 1960s. And my generation (I'm in my 40s) didn't help the situation either; for the most part, we let the escalating colorism slide. Most AAs in my age group did and said nothing as the paper bag test escalated into a manila-folder-and-Whiter test.

I just praise God that you got through all of that and are coming to a healthier sense of self. And you're doing so early in life. There are so many of us who go to our graves being ashamed of our heritage. God is good!

Thank you for your courage in talking HONESTLY about all of this. I will post this tonight (with your name deleted, of course).

Peace and blessings, Khadija

I thought about that e-mail. I'm old enough to be this young lady's mother. It sickens me to know that *this* situation is the collective inheritance that African-American women in my age group left for her and others.

Sometimes younger women don't believe me when I tell them this, but the colorism was not this bad in the early 1980s. I've been speaking out about colorism since I was in high school back then. Over the years, very few other voices joined me. It has gotten worse since I was in high school. It has gotten a thousand times worse since the reign of Black Exploitation Television and hip-hop videos. Most Black women in my age group did and said nothing.

Unless we commit ourselves to cultivating and protecting our own racial and ethnic self-respect, this is the legacy that we will leave for any children we have.

PART II: THE SOJOURNER'S PASSPORT TO SAVING YOUR OWN LIFE

CHAPTER 6

'ALL COLORED PEOPLE THAT WANT TO GO TO KANSAS, ON 9/5/1877, CAN DO SO FOR $5'

Pioneering

If you want something that you've never had, you'll probably have to do something that you've never done—often, without anyone to guide you by the hand. Historically, African-Americans have stepped out on faith. We can do it again. We are descended from people who were willing to step out into the unknown in hopes of better lives.

We've run for our lives before.

We ran from the rural South to Southern cities. We ran from the South to the North. We ran from the South to the West. Some of us ran all the way to Canada. The title of this essay comes from an 1877 notice that advertised the availability of land in Nicodemus, Graham County, Kansas, and encouraged African-Americans to migrate to the state. Nicodemus was settled in 1877, and is the only surviving all-Black settlement west of the Mississippi that was settled by former slaves during the Exoduster period after the Civil War. It is now a historic site administered by the National Park Service.

Sometimes It's Best to Run and Not Look Back

I wonder if we've forgotten how to run for our lives. I'm perplexed by some of the reactions when I say that Black people who want to survive *and* thrive must evacuate Black residential areas. To use secular terms, what used to be the Black community has disintegrated far beyond the point of no return. To use a term that I've heard Christians use, Black residential areas are *filled* with satanic strongholds that are not being pulled down anytime soon. In fact, most of the residents have (at minimum) a passive investment in current conditions remaining as they are. Many of us have a passive investment in supporting the behaviors that prop up these evil strongholds.

Maybe I should list some of the passive investments that I've seen. There is the widespread acceptance of the sexual exploitation of underage Black girls. There is the widespread acceptance of illegitimacy. There is the widespread acceptance of obscene and self-degrading "music." There is the fake religiosity that only gets excited about condemning *the activities that we have no interest in participating in*, such as foaming at the mouth about gays and lesbians. I can't count the numbers of shacked-up baby mammas and baby daddies I've heard who love to rant about gay people. They usually get quiet when I mention that they are shacked up with illegitimate children.

In short, Black people have turned Black residential areas into "sundown towns" where one must be behind locks and gates by sundown. **The greatest danger to any individual Black person's life is often to be found inside Black residential areas.** Is our reluctance to leave because we still haven't figured this out? Or is it something else? Could it be that our popular culture and our (mis-) leaders have encouraged us to confuse *pantomiming* the gestures of pulling down strongholds with actually pulling them down? **Confusing pantomime with the real thing puts us in grave danger.**

It's Not Wise to Tamper with Strongholds Unless You're Prepared for the Backlash

It's not good for people to start things when they're not prepared to deal with the consequences. There are always consequences, even when you are doing the right thing. **Especially when you are doing the right thing.** I've seen more than a few Black Christians who are enamored with the idea of trying to cast out demons, even when they are not prepared for the backlash. This is unwise.

There are many unfortunate examples of this in the worldly realm. For example, I often think about the martyred Dawson family of Baltimore, Maryland, when Black folks talk about "community organizing" as the solution to the criminal threat. Unless folks are coming together to hire armed, professional security forces, they are putting their lives at risk. Angela Dawson, her husband, and her five children were engulfed in flames and died after drug dealers firebombed their home. Mrs. Dawson had alerted police to the drug dealers who loitered and sold drugs in front of her home. The murder of the Dawson family is one of many atrocities caused by the "stop snitchin'" hip hop crack house culture that has infected too many African-Americans.

Too many Black activists make it sound as if dealing with Black criminals is the same as it was on an episode of *Good Times* or *Welcome Back Kotter.* As if all will be right with the world after a few hugs and a few kind words. No.

The Dawson family was martyred because they didn't know that African-American criminals have much in common with the vicious, violent, armed-to-the-teeth warlords in Somalia, and the deranged child soldiers in other parts of Africa. In fact, many of these juvenile criminals *are* child soldiers, with all the evil and depravity that is implied by that term.

The Dawson family needed armed intervention from professional security forces, not community activism. This is what people and businesses that understand reality do: hire professional, armed security. They don't have marches. They understand that the police are generally not going to be proactive in defense of the public. Instead, they will react after something negative has happened. Most hospitals in the Chicago area hire off-duty Chicago police officers as security. These off-duty officers are armed and are fully licensed to arrest people.

Let's be clear. Conditions have reached the point that when folks say you should stay in Black residential areas to "help the community," they are asking you to remain in a Rwanda-like zone. They are usually asking you to live in these zones as an unarmed civilian, who is either a sitting duck or a moving target. (Most "stay and help the community" believers are strictly anti-guns.)

Sometimes, it's best to run and not look back. I believe that all Black people that want to survive and thrive can do so if they are willing to run for their lives.

FOR FURTHER READING: Check out the link to information about Benjamin "Pap" Singleton (1809-1892). Pap knew what to do! And he was dauntless. We weren't so helpless 130 years ago. http://www.pbs.org/weta/thewest/people/s_z/singleton.htm

CHAPTER 7

REALITY CHECK: WHAT THE BLACK UNDERCLASS IS REALLY ALL ABOUT

For too many of us, ideology has replaced reality. This problem has many manifestations. One of which is that we continue to re-gurgitate ideological talking points when confronted with real life situations that are contrary to the ideology. I mentioned the ideo-logical fantasy of a rainbow coalition in an earlier post. Hanging on to this ideology for far too long has damaged Black people's political and economic fortunes in this country.

Hanging on to our romanticized, often abstract view of the Black underclass *will continue to cost Black lives.* Maybe this mass fantasy will ultimately cost you your life. Or the life of a loved one. We don't see the Black underclass as they really are. Instead, we see talking points. Usually talking points that effectively blame "the evil White man." Yes, there are plenty of racist, evil White men, many of whom are in positions of authority.

However, the reality is that you (and anybody you care about) are much more likely to be killed by your "brother." You are much more likely to be carjacked by your so-called brother. You are much more likely to be gang-raped by your "brother." What I find amazing is that we even blame "the evil White man" for the actions of our "kin." I guess most of us don't believe in free will. Even more amazing is our willful refusal to acknowledge that the killers, carjackers, and gang-rapists among us are mostly produced by a particular demographic: the Black underclass.

It's taboo to say this out loud. We encourage one another to demonize and bash the Black middle and upper classes. These people generally aren't killing, robbing, and raping the rest of us. But the Black underclass is a sacred cow that we must pity and rescue, even as they prey on the rest of us. This is insane.

I've worked as a prosecutor. I've spent a much longer period of time as a defense attorney. The vast majority of defendants come from the Black poor and the Black underclass. I've had cases in local criminal, child support, and child protection courtrooms. I've been paying close attention to the defendant population over the years. I've noticed patterns with them. Before somebody screams, let me be clear. I'm not saying that the following description is representative of the Black poor. There's a difference between the Black poor and the Black underclass. Many poor Black people are the working poor who are striving for a better life. However, the Black underclass is distinct from the rest of the Black population.

1. They generally hate other Black people. If you are a Black person who works for a living, they hate you.

2. If you work for a living, they see you as potential prey or as a potential host body to be exploited.

3. They interpret kindness as weakness.

4. They don't want to work for a living, and will go to great lengths to avoid it. They will migrate to states that offer the most generous welfare benefits. To get more free money, many of the women will eagerly have their children labeled and stigmatized as emotionally disturbed. You see, SSI pays "crazy money" benefits to people caring for "crazy" children.

5. They will avail themselves of any free resources, even if this endangers other people. I know of people who set fire to their own Section 8-paid-for apartments to receive new replacement

furniture from social service agencies.

6. They have an aversion to rational thought.

7. Many of them have physical impediments that hinder their cognitive abilities. Scores of them were born with various problems such as fetal alcohol syndrome, and defects related to drug exposure. In addition, many have negative genetic inheritances such as low IQs and predispositions for mental illness.

8. They live for drama and believe that any and every setting is an appropriate stage for acting out their drama.

9. For all of their boldness in disrespecting and harming other Black people, they are **deeply** afraid of White authority figures. This is unlike some Latino defendants who have been bold enough to attack White law enforcement officers and, occasionally, the judge. If we're going to be honest, we really need to give some Latino criminals the "Original American Gangster" award. When you come from countries where it's common for criminals to shoot down law enforcement and judges in volume, I guess American courtrooms aren't all that intimidating. By contrast, I've watched many Black men immediately assume the prisoner stance when in any type of courtroom: hands clasped behind their backs, heads down, and careful to never look White judges and opposing lawyers in the face.

10. The women prefer the "sanctified" type of church. When in prison, the men prefer Islam.

11. Those who have committed crimes have **no** empathy for their victims, and no remorse. The fake remorse only comes after they've been arrested. Before they are arrested, they enjoy the cell phone videos they take of their exploits. **Other people's suffering is a source of pleasure and entertainment.**

12. They view themselves as victims—no matter what. The killers I've represented viewed themselves as victims. The pedophiles I've represented viewed themselves as victims. The mothers who've allowed their children to be molested viewed themselves as victims. Everything is always all about them. No matter what

they have done, they see themselves as the *true* victims in every situation. When you view them as victims, you reinforce their worldview.

What too many well-meaning Black people fail to understand is that the Black underclass is often the moral equivalent of "the evil White man." **When you give blind support to, and make excuses for, the Black underclass, you are often choosing the Janjaweed over the Klan.** Both of these groups are a threat to the rest of us. It's long past time for us to wake up and recognize reality.

CHAPTER 8

THE END OF THE ROAD FOR AFRICAN-AMERICANS, PART 1: THERE IS NO 'BLACK COMMUNITY'

Faith, blog host of *Acts of Faith in Love and Life*, held an important conversation about the existence (or not) of the "Black community," as well as our various understandings of what "community" means.

http://actsoffaithinloveandlife.blogspot.com/2009/07/black-community-what-black-community.html

Instead of taking up undue space in her comment section, I decided to reply with my own blog essay.

My beliefs about this topic are straightforward. There is *no* "Black community." What African-Americans previously had were quasi-communities largely held together by the outside pressures of Jim Crow. During the 1960s, we had the ingredients in place to create fully functional communities. We squandered that opportunity. There won't be any Black communities in the future. Instead, there will be even more deplorable examples of what we currently have: ghettos, slums, and hoods.

All of this has implications for our collective future. It's also partly why African-Americans are forming a *permanent* underclass in this country. For now, let's review some criteria regarding functional communities. I believe that Dr. Claud Anderson has offered the best summary of the ingredients needed for a functional community. He discussed these ingredients in his book, *PowerNomics: The National Plan to Empower Black America*.

The first necessary ingredient Dr. Anderson mentioned was an independent economy that can supply community members with their daily needs, services, and jobs. It's obvious that the African-American business economy can't provide any of this. Let that sink in for a moment. *This* situation is even less functional than the relationship between the colonialist and the colonized. We can't supply a *single one* of our own needs.

The next necessary ingredient, according to Dr. Anderson, is a group code of conduct. African-Americans have this upside-down and backwards. Not only do many of us reject *the idea* of having standards of behavior, but we also enable and reward other Black people for doing things (like committing crimes) that hurt our group's interests. Furthermore, the institutions that would normally assist in establishing codes of conduct (such as families, churches, and schools) have collapsed in Black residential areas. Most African-American houses of worship are corrupt, ineffective, or both. With the absence of marriage and an out-of-wedlock birthrate of over 70 percent, we don't have families anymore. And our "grassroots" have systematically destroyed the public schools that most of us use as free baby-sitters for our poorly raised, often out-of-control children.

Let's contrast the African-American aversion to standards with an example of how some other groups enforce a code of conduct that helps their group's interests. Neil Gabler's book, *An Empire of Their Own: How the Jews Invented Hollywood*, described how Jack Warner (of Warner Bros.) required his Jewish employees to donate a percentage of their salary to Jewish charities.

One reason Mr. Warner was able to do this was because he

produced and provided jobs for his own people. He was able to provide jobs because his own group supported his business. This example of support is in stark contrast to African-American consumers' general refusal to support African-American businesses, which is discussed in Chapter 33.

Another reason Mr. Warner got away with pressuring employees to support Jewish charities was because there was apparently a consensus among Jewish-Americans that this was a reasonable expectation—the expectation that Jewish people would do what they could to support Jewish causes. This is based on having a group code of conduct. All of these things form a positive behavior cycle that African-Americans have never been able to grasp. We generally want to shield destructive Blacks from being punished. Typically, we go so far as to support and reward such persons.

The final necessary ingredient for Dr. Anderson's functional community is political self-government. It's obvious that African-Americans are steadily losing what little political representation that we have. It's no longer only Whites that we allow to rule over us. We now allow Latinos to serve as our political overlords (see Los Angeles and Miami). Recently, African-American fools in Louisiana allowed America's first Vietnamese-American member of Congress to be elected in their majority-Black district.

A review of these necessary ingredients makes it obvious that we don't have Black communities, and that we're not ever going to have them. The necessary building blocks for a functional community are *long gone*, and they're not coming back. The notion of a functioning Black community is yet another rotting corpse in the graveyard of dead cultural and political ideas. May it rest in peace.

Let's stop camping out in the graveyard of various dead ideas, and instead seek to live among the living. Are you ready to pack up your sleeping bag and leave the cemetery? Are you ready to be among the living?

CHAPTER 9

THE END OF THE ROAD FOR AFRICAN-AMERICANS, PART 2: GENERATION(S) APATHETIC

Let's examine some of the voices of advancement, commitment, and ethnic and racial pride among us. In 2006, radio talk show host, café owner, and long-term Black activist Bob Law launched a "Bring Back Black" (BBB) movement. Dr. Claud Anderson's Harvest Institute published an open letter from Mr. Law in its Winter 2006 report, available here:

www.harvestinstitute.org/harvest institute winter 2006.pdf

Dr. Anderson and Mr. Law discussed the BBB Movement in a video accessible here:

http://www.youtube.com/watch?v=mHPcHj21yJ0

I agree with what Bob Law said in his open letter, and most of what he said in the video clip. However, there's a critical part of the equation that he left out of his analysis.

What Mr. Law left out of his analysis is that most African-Americans don't want to "bring Black back." If he wants us to do so, perhaps we should consider who threw Black away in the first place.

We did! The ugly reality is that we never wanted "Black" to begin with! There was never any widespread ethnic or racial self-respect among African-Americans. And we don't want to have any now. That's why we have so many African-Americans clamoring to have themselves and their children considered *anything but Black* (biracial, multi-whatever and Cablanasian).

The honorable battles that Mr. Law, Dr. Anderson, and other elders continue to fight were lost several generations ago. At some point, those of us who value maintaining our ethnic and racial self-respect have to realize that the masses of African-Americans have *no* interest in any of that. At some point, you have to recognize that the customers are refusing to buy what you're selling.

It's important to note that modern generations of African-Americans have even less interest in having ethnic or racial pride than previous generations. Please note the age of most voices of African-American and Black self-respect. These voices include Bob Law, Dr. Claud Anderson, Conrad Worrill, Molefi Asante, Dr. Frances Cress Welsing, Drs. Julia and Nathan Hare, and others. Almost anybody you can name who supports a vision of specifically Black anything is over the age of forty. In fact, most of them are in their sixties and above.

As I see it, the problem isn't their age. The problem is that younger African-Americans have not taken up their mantle and replaced them. That's one way to identify dying and dead cultural movements—there are no young people involved.

To be honest, most African-Americans in my age group (forties) and younger haven't been interested in anything. At all. **A more accurate name for all of us is "Generation(s) Apathetic."** This mass apathy, *especially* toward anything involving specifically Black and African-American issues, is the reason any plan that depends on our mass participation is doomed to failure. The only mass phenomena among African-Americans will be continued mass apathy, increasing mass casualties, and permanent mass underclass status.

There can be, and are, small groupings of like-minded people among us who will escape, survive, and thrive.

However, *generations of apathy* mean that mass Black mobilization is yet another dead political and cultural idea. The notion of mobilizing to save all of our people is a rotting corpse. May it rest in peace.

Let's stop camping out in the graveyard of various dead ideas, and instead seek to live among the living. Are you ready to pack up your sleeping bag and leave the cemetery? Are you ready to be among the living?

CHAPTER 10

THE LAST EMBERS OF A DYING FLAME: WILL YOU MAKE IT OUT BEFORE DARKNESS FALLS?

Various Black women-empowerment bloggers have given clear warnings about what's coming. Those who have the courage to acknowledge reality can see for themselves that the emerging *endless night of permanent underclass status* is almost upon African-Americans. We've been watching the last embers of a dying flame before it finally flickers out.

Some of us have already used what's left of the light to flee to other places where it still shines brightly, and where there is still warmth. With halting, hesitant steps, some of us are still making our way out of the *African-American social anarchy and chaos zones* while the light still flickers. **Such people need to pick up their pace.** Unfortunately, most of us are still aimlessly chattering about trivial things. Or chattering about saving other, less fortunate people when we are still in a precarious position. **Such people are already dead.** They just don't know it yet.

That *final* moment of weak, flickering light before complete darkness is now upon us.

The campfires and hearths that our ancestors kept burning, the cultural warmth that protected us from madness, violence and depravity, are about to go out. For the last time. They won't be reignited.

African-American residential and social dungeons are already terrible, **deadly** places. And this is *with* the dying embers still giving off a bit of light and warmth. When the fire dies, the resulting frozen, dark vacuum will destroy all who remain within.

For those African-American women who are still confused, here's a situation report.

The Source of the Problem Is Obvious

As women, we really do know the source of our collective problems. We've simply been obeying the cultural taboo against speaking this truth out loud. The source of most African-American women's major, life-damaging, life-threatening problems comes from:

- *Non-reciprocating* African-American men, who constitute the overwhelming majority of African-American men
- African-American women's involvement and interactions with *non-reciprocating* African-American men
- African-American women's quest to be involved and interact with *non-reciprocating* African-American men

Non-reciprocating African-American men, and our interactions or involvement with them, are the root cause of most of our serious problems as African-American women. I will add that these men are only able to cause these problems with African-American women's complicity and cooperation.

The Solution Is Equally Obvious

The solution is for African-American women to disconnect

from these men. This will solve roughly 90 percent of their serious problems.

Physical and Emotional Safety. Once you remove yourself from Black residential areas, you'll be physically safer. That's because you won't be around African-American males who are shooting bullets in all directions. You won't be around African-American male carjackers, and other violent criminals. Your spirit will also be safer because you won't be subjected to African-American males' street harassment of Black women.

Self-Confidence. Once you stop socializing in settings filled with African-American males, your self-confidence as a woman will probably rise. This is because when you get out into the wider world, you'll see that normal men are attracted to women in general—including Black women like you. The interesting thing that I've noticed about nonracist men from other groups is that, as far as they are concerned, all visibly Black woman are equally Black. Nonracist men from other groups are not measuring Black women's noses, lips, and hair textures like many colorist Black men.

Resources Available for Your Own Aspirations. Once you stop supporting African-American males' causes (such as Oscar Grant, and scholarships for Black males), you'll have more time, energy, and money available for your own aspirations.

Peace of Mind. Once you stop interacting with African-American males *unless they are contributing something of value to your life*, you'll have more peace of mind. You won't be subjected to their verbal abuse and denigration of African-American women. Once you stop consuming entertainment products from African-American men in general, your spirits will naturally rise. Cutting the cord on non-reciprocating African-American males (who make up the majority of African-American males) will naturally solve most of African-American women's problems. The rest will be solved by some intensive introspection and internal work.

Placing Self-Created Obstacles on the Escape Route

More than a few African-American women can see the need to get out while the light is still flickering, but choose to place obstacles in their own escape path. They do things that hinder their ability to exit the chaos zones. Here are some examples:

Engaging in Defeminizing and Self-Stigmatizing Behavior. This can range from the public cursing that many of us irrationally insist won't harm our image, to the various other stigmatizing banners we affix to our foreheads. Such banners include the *"Sympathize With My Obesity Because I'm Traumatized And Emotionally Disturbed"* banner, the *"I Should Be Able to Let It ALL Hang Out"* banner, the *"Therapy Talk"* banner, and the *"I Would Never Date or Marry Outside My Race"* banner. Tell the truth—if a White person said this in public you would consider them to be racist. What makes you think others aren't having similar reactions when you blurt this out?

Refusing to Work on Maintaining a Healthy Weight. A woman needs to have as many different cards she can play as possible. Including the health card—which is endangered by being overweight—and the physical-attraction card. Study after study has documented the effect of a person's perceived looks on various situations. Why do you think there hasn't been a hideous presidential candidate after the television era began? Ugly individuals like Abraham Lincoln would **never** be elected to any office today. I'm not talking about what's fair or right, I'm talking about reality. Any condition that distances one from what is commonly considered attractive needs to be worked on.

Continuing to Hitch One's Fate to African-American Men. This makes no sense at all. Many African-American women act as if we're the ones that are in a weaker position. Many (if not most) African-American males only subsist because we support them. We are the life support that makes their existence possible. If African-American women finally pull the plug on non-reciprocating African-American males, most of them will cease to exist.

African-American women are the ones that are most functional within our ethnic collective. African-American males cannot support their own needs, whether it's their protest-march needs or anything else. Black women are the majority of the foot soldiers for the civil rights organizations that meet Black males' protest needs. African-American women are the majority of the foot soldiers for *all* of these Black groups (the NAACP, the National Action Network) except for the Nation of Islam. I suspect that one reason the Nation of Islam is an exception to this pattern is because they heavily recruit from the prisons.

Why are so many of us acting as if we're the ones who are needy and radioactive in terms of personal survival? It must be the brainwashing that we have bought into. This learned helplessness is the result of listening to the confidence- and soul-killing slander that African-American men have committed against us.

However, their slander is not reality. The reality is that, unlike most African-American males, African-American women have the ability *and* the resources to walk away into healthier environments. We just have to get up and leave. It's that simple. At least it's that simple while the last ember is still burning. It's simple while that last bit of light is still flickering.

Stop Looking Back at 'Sodom'

I was amazed by the *shocked—shocked I say!*—outrage about the latest atrocity on Black Exploitation Television. I feel that this particular outrage (the alleged airing of what comes close to simulated child pornography during the 2009 BET Awards show) was yet another sign.

There were those people who could still be lured to turn back and look at Sodom/BET. Just like Lot's wife looked back at Sodom in the Bible. She was supposedly running from the impending destruction of Sodom to save her life. But she looked back, and was turned into a pillar of salt. I guess the point of that story is that, to survive, she was supposed to run away from that place and never look back.

I believe the disgusting spectacle that BET tricked many people into watching (with false promises of some sort of tribute to Michael Jackson) was a warning. It was one of the final warnings about the folly of continuing to "look back" and consume popular "Black" culture—for any reason whatsoever.

And then there are other people who cannot be lured to turn back and look upon Sodom/BET. People who fled or are running from Sodom and refuse to look back. For any reason.

I would strongly urge you to *stop* looking back at "Sodom."

- Don't look back at BET-Sodom.
- Don't look back at the "White Girl Song"-Sodom that Black bloggers have discussed.
- Don't look back at the Internet Ike Turners' blogs-Sodom or the Internet Ike Turners' YouTube videos-Sodom. (Head scarf flutter in salute to blogger Gina McCauley, blog host of *What About Our Daughters* for coining the phrase "Internet Ike Turner.")
- Don't look back at entertainment products from Damaged Beyond Repair Black Men (DBRBM)-Sodom.

Stop looking back at Sodom! God has let you slide for now. In His Grace, He has granted you a few more moments to make it out to safety. A few more moments to get clear of Sodom. But eventually you *will* be turned into a metaphorical pillar of salt if you continue to look back at what He does not want you to take in. **You can't run forward while looking backward!**

It's now or never for those African-American women who intend to escape and survive. Will *you* make it out in time?

DOMESTIC VIOLENCE: YOU DON'T NEED ANYBODY'S PERMISSION TO SAVE YOUR OWN LIFE—JUST DO IT

A reader asked me to speak out about the recent news of a Pakistani-American Muslim who allegedly beheaded his wife in upstate New York. Muzzammil Hassan, who founded a cable television station to promote better understanding of Muslims in the U.S., was arrested on charges he beheaded his wife, Aasiya Hassan.

I was initially hesitant to discuss this particular story because I wasn't sure I had anything useful to say about it. But the more I thought, I decided there are a few reality-check aspects to domestic violence that usually aren't mentioned or emphasized in most discussions about this issue.

If You Are a Victim of Domestic Violence, Don't Expect Support from 'Friends,' Family, or Especially Religious Leaders

The harsh reality is that we live in a culture of widespread support for violence against women. That culture includes *women who support violence against other women*. This is especially true for Black women.

So, if you need to save your own life, *don't* count on support from so-called friends or family. The odds are that you won't receive it from them. It is *almost certain* that you won't receive support from religious leaders. Many ministers and imams are batterers themselves. **Don't ask these people for permission to save your own life. Just do it.**

Unfortunately, the public (which can include *your* relatives and acquaintances) is **filled** with people who support, enable, and excuse violence against women.

If You Offer Help to a Victim of Domestic Violence, Do So from a Safe Distance

This is the part where I'm sure to offend many, if not most, survivors of domestic violence. I must admit that I'm not automatically as empathetic as I used to be about this issue. I've had too much work-related exposure to domestic violence victims, both as a former prosecutor and as a defense attorney.

Here's the part that women's advocates won't tell you:

Many women who are victims of domestic violence will ultimately, and eagerly, go back to their abusers. If you allowed yourself to get heavily involved in "rescuing" such a woman, she and her abuser will paint you as somebody who just wanted to break them up (after she returns to him). This means that the male abuser might want to come after you after they are lovey-dovey again!

Many women who are victims of domestic violence will also destroy any sanctuary that you offer them. They will bring predators into the previously safe environment. After she reconciles with the man who beats her, she will start having him come visit her in the new apartment that you provided for her. She will be resentful if you won't allow him to move in with her. This has happened to several other landlords I know.

Good Samaritan, beware!

CHAPTER 12

DEMOGRAPHICS ARE DESTINY: WHAT WENT WRONG WITH ORTHODOX SUNNI BLACK MUSLIMS

The Contrast Between the Nation of Islam (NOI) and Orthodox Sunni African-American Muslims

I am an orthodox Sunni Muslim. I have never been a member of the Nation of Islam. So my critique of (and disgust with) Sunni Black Muslims is coming from *inside* this category, not outside.

As vehemently as I disagree with what I believe are the false religious teachings of the NOI (such as preaching that God Almighty "appeared in the person of Master W. Fard Muhammad, July 1930"), I have to give credit where credit is due. I have to give credit for the NOI's good works within Black residential areas. Meanwhile, we Sunni Black Muslims have next to none.

I have to give credit for the ethnic self-respect that is taught within the NOI. Meanwhile, we Sunni Black Muslims generally have next to none. In fact, there's at least one Sunni Black Muslim imam preaching that Arabs are a superior race. Abdur-Rahman Muhammad, blog host of *A Singular Voice (which can be found at http://singularvoice.wordpress.com/)*, did a post exposing one Black slave-mentality imam in particular who preaches this doctrine.

I have to give credit to the NOI's ability to lift their followers out of poverty through economic teachings. Meanwhile, we Sunni Black Muslims often celebrate poverty because of laziness under the guise of being religious students.

I have to give credit to the NOI's proven ability to reform criminals. Meanwhile, we Sunni Black Muslims tend to excuse and ignore criminality among our group—although recent circumstances might force us to stop that for a minute (at least in public). Several Sunni Black Muslim men in the Philadelphia area with luxuriant beards allegedly committed an armed robbery and killed a police officer while wearing women's veils.

I have to give credit to the NOI's demonstrated emphasis on stable, monogamous marriages. Meanwhile, we Sunni Black Muslims have within our group Black men who have literally been married twenty to thirty times, with some "marriages" lasting just a few days. Some Sunni Black Muslims also practice the insanity of polygamy in a modern context.

(I have a suggestion for those Sunni Black Muslims who believe that every social practice mentioned in the Holy Quran was intended to endure forever, as opposed to being phased out as human understanding evolves over time. If you believe that, then why don't you go back to slavery? After all, slavery was also mentioned in the Holy Quran. Nothing is stopping you from becoming an unpaid servant to some Gulf Arabs. Could it be that you only want to preserve those unjust social practices that favor men at the expense of women?)

If only there was a Black Muslim faith community that had the ethnic self-respect and self-discipline of the NOI and legitimate Islamic beliefs.

We Must Resist Immigrant Muslim Domination of Black Muslim Thought

The possibility of religiously approved misogyny is what attracts many African-American men to Islam in the first place. Islam (as practiced) is often the last refuge of aspiring batterers and harem operators. From what I hear and read, this is getting worse with the increasing prevalence of Black Muslim "Ike Turner" imams. This is partially the result of African-American Muslims adopting Arab cultural practices such as extreme misogyny. Many of us mistake Arab and Pakistani tribal culture with Islam itself.

We must oppose immigrant Muslim domination of Black Muslim thought and discourse. The sectarian and extremist modes of thought that Muslim Blacks have copied from immigrant Muslims have had a devastating effect on Muslim Black women and children.

Muslim Black women and children are safer with the Nation of Islam "cult" than within "orthodox" Black Muslim mosques. When Muslim Blacks still did our own thinking, we *never* engaged in the depths of anti-woman and anti-child practices that many of us have now copied from these immigrants. Any effort that undermines the immigrants' control of Black Muslim minds can potentially save Black Muslim women's lives.

As weak and servile as so many orthodox Muslim Black men are in their behavior with racist Arabs and Pakistanis, they are still holding many Muslim Black women and children in their thrall. There are more than a few Muslim Black women who became Muslim to please a man. This sets them up for heavy-duty exploitation. These women and children are often part of a desperately suffering subculture. The depths of their degradation are usually kept hidden from public view. Anything that helps loosen the grip of immigrant-inspired thought on the Black Muslim males who control them will improve these Black women's and children's lives.

Rejecting immigrant Muslim domination is vital to the long-term survival of Islam among African-Americans. As things stand, orthodox Black Muslims are headed for complete disintegration. Transplanting Arab and Pakistani political priorities and versions of Islam to American soil is destroying the African-American ortho-dox Muslim collective. We are losing previous African-American converts to the faith as fast as we gain new ones. We can't form stable, healthy families. Many of our children grow up to run away from anything that calls itself "Islam." These calamities are the re-sult of slavishly imitating foreign Muslims. **We are dominated by immigrant Muslims even though African-American Muslims are roughly *one-third* of all Muslims in the U.S.**

A commenter, Pioneer Valley Woman (blog host of *Episcopalienne*), zeroed in on a huge problem with these immi-grant-influenced Muslim Blacks. Their Arab and Pakistani masters have instructed them that nationalism is bad. However, it only counts as big, bad nationalism when Black Muslims express any concern whatsoever for other Black people.

When these same Arab and Pakistani masters instruct their Black servants to support Arab and Pakistani nationalist projects, this is called "supporting the *ummah*" (the faith community of all Muslims). If it's something that affects the immigrant Muslims or their countries of origin, then this concern is characterized as something that affects *all* Muslims. Meanwhile, if it's something that affects Muslim Blacks' communities of origin (Black residen-tial areas), families of origin, or even ourselves directly, then it's *of no concern*. This is why racial profiling was officially of *no concern* to many immigrant Muslims until these same immigrant Muslims lost their "honorary White" status after the 9/11 terror attacks.

It's similar to the bait and switch that goes on with how Black interests are defined. Black interests equals Black men's inter-ests only. Keeping the idea of reciprocity in mind quickly exposes what's wrong with all of these various lopsided, one-way, and oppressive interactions.

On the subject of reciprocity, these same Palestinians that all Muslims are almost required to support are also many of the "Immigrant Muslim Merchants of Death" who sell crack pipes, marijuana cigarette rolling papers, liquor, and pork in Black residential areas. I also notice that their imams never condemn this behavior. This is part of the reason I'm not obsessed with what's currently going on in Gaza. I do have some compassion for the people of Gaza. But I care about other people to the same extent that they care about me and mine. No more and no less.

Demographics Are Destiny

How did all of this come to be? The answer is found in demographics. I've come to understand that demographics trends are often underlying culture shifts. In this case, several demographic trends combined to create a perfect storm of madness within the orthodox Black American Muslim collective.

The dying off of the old guard among orthodox Black Muslim imams. There was a time when I would guess 98 percent of the Muslim Black imams were men who had come through the old NOI at some point in their lives before they accepted Sunni Islam. My retired imam is one such man. The Arabs and Pakistanis could *never* dominate (or even influence) such Black men. The sense of ethnic self-respect that such imams absorbed while they had been in the NOI inoculated them against undue immigrant influence. Many of these men have retired or passed away during the last decade.

We now have had twenty-five years (and counting) of Black imams who were never part of the NOI. The current generation of Black imams were molded and trained by Pakistanis and Arabs. Many of these African-American men went to Arab countries to study (often on scholarships offered by the Saudi government). As a result, some of these puppet Black imams measure one's devotion to Islam by the degree of one's devotion to those who sit on the Saudi throne!

I would compare the situation to the rise of crossover Black politicians who never came up through any Black-controlled move-ment activities. Crossover Black politicians *like President Obama and others who were never trained under Black-led movements, Black activists, or any Black people in general.* I firmly believe that African-Americans are going to reap a similar whirlwind from these crossover Black politicians once all the "old heads" like Rev. "Baby Daddy" Jackson and Rev. "Hot Comb" Sharpton are finally gone from the scene.

There are *grave* problems with these old heads, but they at least responded to some of our needs. For example, who can you call when some White student hangs a noose on your door (besides your lawyer)? Crossover Black politicians don't respond to these sorts of problems.

Anyway, I had no idea of this shift until recent years. I was happy at my mosque. I had been blissfully unaware of this de-mographic shift until my imam retired. That's when I discovered that men like him were not considered mainstream by those Black Muslims who were trained by Arabs and Pakistanis. The common understanding of what is mainstream has shifted because of these underlying demographics. My retired imam is considered a Black Nationalist (which is considered bad) because he does not slav-ishly follow or imitate foreign Muslims.

The current widespread acceptance of criminality among orthodox Black Muslims is another result of demographics. There has been too much emphasis (for too many decades) on recruiting Black male criminals in prison. These recruits form a disproportionate number of the Black male Muslims in almost all mosques. The difference is that the NOI has a firm structure in place to monitor these felons and discipline them for backsliding into criminality. There is no such structure in orthodox Black mosques.

This intersects with the first demographic trend. Old-guard

Black imams who came through the NOI were firm disciplinarians when it came to criminality. Jailbird Muslim Black men tended to avoid mosques run by old-school Black imams because these old-school imams won't tolerate criminal activity. The Arabs and Pakistanis never trained their Black puppet imams to chastise criminals because the spread of criminality among Black Muslims was never one of their concerns. It doesn't matter to them. They know their Black puppet imams will only be allowed to run Black-populated mosques. And it's *not* like they were going to allow their Black male puppets to marry into their families.

Their general refusal to allow their daughters to marry Muslim Black men is one of the popular complaints among orthodox Black Muslim males. This is why many of them fly all the way over to Morocco to buy Arab wives. It's interesting to note that Pakistanis in Pakistan won't play that—*no* amount of money will convince them to allow Black men to marry their daughters.

Eventually, reports of Muslim Black male criminality, drug use, down-low behavior, and other destructive hobbies *will* get back to these villages in Morocco. At which point this avenue of buying non-Black women will be closed to orthodox Muslim Black men. (This situation has gotten so far out of hand that Abdur-Rahman Muhammad, blog host of *A Singular Voice*, wrote a post telling other Sunni Muslim Black men that buying Moroccan women is not the answer.)

Many immigrant-controlled, puppet Black Muslim imams are waiting for Minister Farrakhan to pass away. They would like to take control over Minister Farrakhan's followers (and especially, their money). I will simply urge all NOI members to *beware* of immigrant-dominated orthodox Muslims seeking dialogue with you!

Hijrah from Orthodox African-American Mosques for the Sake of Allah

It's long past time for African-American Sunni Muslim women to flee from African-American Sunni mosques. For the sake of Allah. For the sake of their own lives. For the sake of their children's lives. For the sake of maintaining their Islam.

It's time for those of us who haven't already left to make *hijra* (emigrate) and *move ourselves away from evil* as Allah commands in the Holy Quran. Allah has already stressed to us that His Earth is spacious. Surely, there is a place for us other than among rabid predators.

The widespread corruption and depravity of African-American Sunni Muslim men (*with help from Black Muslim women who enable them*) has reached a point that it is nearly impossible for a sane African-American Muslim woman to practice Islam in safety in most of these mosques. The children are also in grave danger in these mosques. There are many predators, and almost no protectors. This is why, *years* after my former imam retired (who is an honorable man, explaining why he had few followers), I haven't found a mosque that I feel comfortable attending.

It turns out that Muslim Black women and children are *much* safer in the heterodox Nation of Islam, a group that most Sunni Muslims consider to be a non-Muslim cult. Let me repeat for the record that I have never been a member of the Nation of Islam; I am a Sunni Muslimah.

On top of all of this, many of these immigrant-controlled, puppet Black imams encourage irresponsible, highly impressionable Sunni Black Muslim males to run off to places like Yemen to become so-called religious students. (See "Harrowing tales from a Yemen prison," Philadelphia Daily News, April 27, 2009, and "As 2 gained freedom in Yemen, 3rd lost it," Philadelphia Daily News, April 28, 2009.) I don't think it's a random coincidence that Abdulhakim Muhammad, the (presumably Sunni) Black Muslim individual alleged to have recently shot and killed a U.S. Army recruiter, had previously been to Yemen.

Conditions have reached the point that many orthodox Black Muslim men (and the Black Muslim women who enable their evil) are a threat to other Black Muslim women and children. Many orthodox Black Muslims are also a threat to American society in general. For your own safety, it's best to stay away from anywhere such people congregate. Starting with their mosques.

PART III: THE SOJOURNER'S PASSPORT TO FULFILLING RELATIONSHIPS

LET'S GET SERIOUS ABOUT VETTING MEN, PART 1: DO YOU REALLY WANT A FATHERLESS MAN TO BE THE FATHER OF YOUR CHILDREN?

Since this is a meeting for current and aspiring sojourners, I'm not even going to bother discussing the widely-known undesirables that any prudent woman would totally screen out of her romantic life—convicts, drug users, and playboys.

Instead, let's talk about something that I hear very few African-American women mention when they discuss the husband potential of various men: whether or not these men grew up with a father.

I find this quite strange, because the composition of a date's family of origin is one of the first few questions that old-school African-American parents want answers to ("*Who are his people?*"). This is also one of the first few questions that many middle-class African-American parents will have about the people their children date. Parents from many other ethnic groups (such as African; Asian, including South Asian; and Middle Eastern) typically go even further with these inquiries. Parents from these groups tend strongly to discourage their children from dating people from broken or dysfunctional homes. They do this because they understand that their child isn't just marrying an individual, but is actually *marrying into another family's background.*

Modern Western culture likes to characterize such screening as intrusive and cruel, but it's actually quite kind in the long run by sparing people unnecessary problems.

The harsh reality is that most people do what they saw their parent(s) do. The example set by their parent(s) is their default setting, good or bad. So, let's consider this in terms of fatherless men. Let's consider what it might mean if you select a fatherless man to be your husband and the father of your children.

Do you really want your children's father to be a man who:

- Has never seen what a live-in, full-time husband and father does?
- Has never seen a father be a part of everyday routines (like finding their kid's socks or shoes when getting dressed for school)?
- Has never seen a father play an integral role in creating family holiday traditions?
- Has never seen a father put up the family Christmas tree each year?
- Has never helped *his* father put up the family Christmas tree each year?
- Has never seen a father play an integral role in creating family weekend traditions?
- Has never seen a father get up before everybody else in the house to clear the snow off the steps and sidewalk that his family will use to go to school or work that morning?
- Has never seen a father clearing the ice off the windows of his wife's car while doing the above?
- Has never seen a father get up in the middle of the night to walk through the house and peek into various

rooms to make sure the children are safe and sleeping comfortably?

- Has never seen what a healthy, day-to-day relationship between a married couple looks like from *inside* the home?

- Has never seen a husband showing daily respect and consideration for his wife?

- Has never seen a father show daily affection for his children?

- Has never seen a father having and implementing a plan for his children's educational futures?

- Has never seen a father having and implementing a plan for his children's vocational futures?

- Has never seen a father discuss his children's future relationships with them (what is to be looked for and valued in a spouse)?

- Has never seen a man show respect for legitimate authority?

There are countless other, specific questions that I could ask along these lines. But you get the idea. It's something that bears some serious consideration.

Addendum: Before somebody writes in to talk about how President Obama is a fatherless man, let's carefully think about that for a moment. First, common sense should tell us that the exception is not the rule. Common sense should also make it plain that Obama is atypical in *many* ways. Being fatherless and raised by Whites in Hawaii and Indonesia is probably quite different from being fatherless and raised under other conditions in other places. I also suspect that, for political reasons, he has downplayed the role his (Muslim) Indonesian stepfather played in raising him.

Second, there's no *rational* reason to assume that President Obama is such a great father. I know many of us enjoy the symbolism of the publicity photos he takes with his daughters, but let's try to think clearly about this for a moment. I find it interesting that nobody really stops to consider just how absent he's been (due to a political career that he voluntarily chose) during *huge* portions of his young daughters' lives. To a small child, absent is absent.

From previous interviews, his absences seem to have been a source of friction in his marriage. He lightly touched on this himself during his infamous Father's Day speech when he said: *"I say this knowing that I have been an imperfect father—knowing that I have made mistakes and will continue to make more; wishing that I could be home for my girls and my wife more than I am right now."*

Addendum No. 2: The Internet Ike Turners (head scarf flutter in salute to Gina McCauley, blog host of What About Our Daughters for coining that phrase) and Ikettes are losing their minds about *the very idea* of African-American women adhering to universal standards used to evaluate men. So, I see that I'm going to have to enforce accountability for this conversation. This means that I won't post any anonymous comments during this conversation.

Addendum No. 3: These series of posts are about the universal standards used by heterosexual women across the planet to evaluate men as potential husbands and fathers. Fatherlessness also affects girls, but since heterosexual women are not seeking to marry and raise children with other women, the effect of fatherlessness on girls is not relevant to this conversation. Therefore, when interjecting themselves into *women's* conversations about how fatherlessness impacts *potential spouses for themselves*, concerned Internet Ike Turners and Ikettes need to present their concerns about fatherless women at lesbian blogs. It should be elementary to note that lesbians are the only women who would be evaluating fatherless women as potential spouses for themselves!

CHAPTER 14

LET'S GET SERIOUS ABOUT VETTING MEN, PART 2: THE DEFICITS CREATED BY FATHERLESSNESS ARE NOT EQUAL BETWEEN THE GENDERS

During Part 1 of this series, I had the following exchange with a couple of readers that merits repetition:

A reader named Jeanetta said: "Thank you for your post, Khadija. I agree with the premise but wonder how a woman with a questionable family background of her own might go about securing a man with a more desirable family background.

"I am the child of a fatherless father *and* a fatherless mother. (My paternal grandfather died when my dad was two. My mother was the mistress's daughter.) My experience is that absence of a father impacted my mother's parenting skills and her relationship with my father as much as it impacted my father's parenting skills and his relationship with my mother.

"How would you suggest that fatherless women successfully address the concerns that a man with a father (and his family) might have with *her* as a potential mate?"

A reader named Rainebeaux said: "Khadija, I thank you

profusely for this post. Of course, like KM and Jeanetta, I'm sweating buckets re: meeting a man's standards with my background (absentee/deceased father, abysmal track record of marriage on mom's side; mom/dad never married, etc.)

"Looking forward to future responses..."

In reply, I said: "Jeanetta, I'm going to be blunt here, please bear with me. This is because time is *very* short for those few AA women who will make it out and create better futures for themselves and their children. So, there's no more time to beat around the bush or walk on eggshells about certain things.

"Respectfully, the very premises and assumptions that seem to underlie your question show that you've been hoodwinked and bamboozled. Here's what I mean: Unless you come from a family background of drug addicts and convicts, why would you think that you're in a comparable situation to a fatherless male when being evaluated?

"It's interesting. Whenever deficits are discussed, African-American male protectionists like to pretend that deficits are "equal" in how they play out for each gender. No, they're not.

"Unless their mothers were also absent (or negligent), most fatherless women have seen a woman (their own mothers) perform *large* portions of a mother's role.

"This means that fatherless women have learned most of the things that go into performing their own future role—the role of being a mother.

"Meanwhile, fatherless men have not seen a man perform any, much less large, portions of a father's role. This means that fatherless men have not learned most of the things that go into performing their own future role—the role of being a father.

"Now, fatherless women often have problems on the "wife front" (since they haven't seen that part of the role modeled), but they're much less likely to make fundamental errors in terms of knowing how to mother children. Because by watching their own mothers, they've seen up close and personal how mothering works in action.

"This is in sharp contrast to the fundamental errors that many fatherless men make in terms of being a father to their own children (such as believing that minimal fatherhood duties are heroic expectations, and believing that weekend, long-distance, and telephone-based fathering is OK). They make these fundamental errors because they've never seen fathering in action.

"So, Jeanetta, If your mother worked for a living to put food on your table, etc...

"If your mother kept you adequately bathed, clothed, and sheltered...

"If your mother cooked for you...

"If your mother combed your hair every day...

"If your mother helped you with your homework...

"If your mother took care of your emotional needs...

"If your mother did the million and one things that are involved in day-to-day child care and childrearing...

"Then you have a pretty good idea of what's normal, and how to perform your future role as a mother!

"The only thing that I could see raising a comparable number of red flags is if you didn't have the opportunity while growing up to see how being a mother works on an everyday, up-close-and-personal basis. This sort of thing generally only applies to girls who grow up with absent or negligent mothers (dope fiend mothers, convict mothers, lazy welfare queen mothers, etc.). Peace, blessings and solidarity."

In response, Rainebeaux said: "Khadija: ohhhh...I've seen moms in action, doing same. Got it. It's mostly the BM—most of whom disqualify themselves, as you've touched on in the post—giving us this kind of grief, demanding that we jump through the flaming hoops! I see this more clearly now."

"Yes, pretending that the effects of fatherlessness are somehow equal between genders is a dishonest trickbag."

The bottom line? Ladies, stop grading African-American men on a curve, and start doing what's best for your future children! Nobody is grading *you* on a curve. And no other ethnic group of women on this planet grades men on a curve—including other types of Black women, such as African women. (I borrowed the phrase "grading Black men on a curve" from an extremely astute blogger named Focused Purpose. Thanks, Sis!)

CHAPTER 15

LET'S GET SERIOUS ABOUT VETTING MEN, PART 3: SCREEN OUT MEN WHO SAY THAT WOMEN WON'T LET THEM BE MEN OR GENTLEMEN

As we continue with this series, one thing you'll notice is that I'm talking about objective traits here—things that have nothing to do with race, color, ethnicity, religion, or other trivialities.

I'm talking about universal standards of quality versus lack of quality. Universal standards that women from every ethnic group (other than African-American women) have always applied. Universal standards that have stood the test of time. Any African-American woman who wants a good life for herself and her children will have to start using universal standards for screening men as potential husbands and fathers. And they will have to stop grading African-American men (or anybody else) on a curve. I will note that nobody is grading *you* on a curve.

Another thing you'll notice is the traits that mark inferior men often go hand in hand and reinforce each other. When you screen out a man based on one low-quality trait, you're usually screening out a man who has a *cluster of other inferior traits*—some of which you simply haven't found out about yet.

As we discussed in Part 1 of this series, a woman is inviting trouble and a low quality of life for her unborn children when she chooses a fatherless man as a husband. As we'll see during this conversation, a woman is also inviting the same thing when she chooses a man who makes the following sorts of statements: *"Women won't let a man be a man,"* *"Women won't let me be a man,"* *"Women won't let a man be a gentleman,"* or *"Women won't let me be a gentleman."*

These sorts of statements reflect an overall mind-set, but it's a weak and conquered one. It's a mind-set that makes it extremely unlikely for the man speaking this weakness to be an effective protector and provider for any woman who's foolish enough to try to build a family with him. And it's a mind-set that is *the opposite* of a quality man's mind-set.

First, somebody who's telling you that somebody else (who-ever it may be—women, men from other ethnic or racial groups, the Devil) won't let him be a man or a gentleman is already tell-ing you that he's not a man or gentleman. Why would you waste time with somebody who's telling you that he's not a man or a gentleman?

Second, the man who speaks this weakness has surrendered control over *his* manhood or status as a gentleman to *somebody else*. You need to ask yourself, "What else has he surrendered control over?"

The men who speak the this weakness are often the same men who say that other people:

- Won't let them earn a living
- Won't let them get an education
- Won't let them learn a trade
- Won't let them learn a skill

Even more dangerous for your future children, these also tend to be the men who say that other people (*the children's mothers, the White man, the Devil, whoever*) won't let them be fathers to their own children!

It's Your Choice: A Powerless Man or an Effective Man as the Father of Your Children

Do you really want a man with a powerless mind-set to be the father of your children? Not if you have any sense.

Quality Men Have Self-Efficacy: The Belief that They Can Make Things Happen

African-Americans with old-school values don't need to administer a psychological test to measure these sorts of things. We know weak minds when we see them! But since so many modern African-Americans have never been exposed to old-school ways of recognizing inferior traits, I feel the need to discuss one modern, scientific measure in detail.

There are psychological tests that measure a person's sense of powerlessness. One of them is called the General Self-Efficacy Scale. The scale was created to assess a general sense of perceived self-efficacy with the aim of predicting a person's ability to cope with daily difficulties as well as adaptation after experiencing stressful life events. The scale is usually self-administered as part of a more comprehensive questionnaire. Typically, the ten statements are mixed in with a larger set of questions. The person chooses a numbered response to describe how accurately each statement describes their beliefs about themselves. Some examples of the statements are, "I can always manage to solve difficult problems if I try hard enough" and "If someone opposes me, I can find the means and ways to get what I want."

Is believing that *"women won't let me be a man or gentleman"* consistent with having the *"I can make things happen"* mind-set of the above statements? No, it's not. A man believing that women (or anybody else) control his manhood or ability to be a gentleman is the exact opposite of having the beliefs mentioned in the General Self-Efficacy Scale. That sort of mental weakness is the very opposite of having any self-efficacy.

There are several intersecting points about the modern prevalence of males manifesting this sort of mental weakness. First, it's often an example of how mass fatherlessness has distorted many African-Americans' perceptions of what's normal masculine behavior. Normal, functional, effective men don't whine about what other people won't "let" them do. That telltale phrase of "they won't let me" isn't even in a normal man's vocabulary.

What normal, functional, effective men will say are things like, "So-and-so doesn't want me to do A. But I got around that by doing B." Or "So-and-so doesn't want me to do X. But I'm going to get around that by doing Y."

Women who have had the misfortune to spend their entire lives surrounded by weak men often don't know this. The functional and effective Black men I've known laugh at the men who talk that talk. They laugh, and scornfully call them "punks" and "busters." (If you don't know, look it up in an online urban dictionary.)

Second, it's an example of how deficits are not equal in how they play out between the genders. I don't like to hear people speak powerlessness. This does not mean that I engage in, or favor, "Superwoman" talk. Just because you can do something doesn't mean that you should do it. It also doesn't mean that it's good to announce that you can do it.

However, if there's going to be an outward display of a degree of powerlessness, the (powerless) damsel in distress plays much better than the (powerless) male in distress. It's acceptable and within normal gender roles for a woman to allow a man to protect and provide for her, and to "rescue" her. It's not acceptable or normal for a man to look for women to rescue him, or prop up his faltering manhood.

The men who fail in performing the normal responsibilities of manhood (being effective protectors and providers for the women and children within their orbit) are typically the ones who make these they-won't-let-me statements. Failed men also often engage in dysfunctional fake-masculine behaviors such as violence and extreme promiscuity.

A sensible woman will choose a husband who knows that he can make good things happen for his family. You don't want a mentally weak man to be the father of your children. When you hear a man speaking weakness and powerlessness, just walk away. Don't get angry or argue with the men who speak that weakness out loud. Be happy that these men are telling on themselves so you can quickly eliminate them from the list of potential husbands and fathers. There's no time to waste.

Many African-American women are resistant to setting minimal standards, much less universal standards used by women from every other ethnic group—including African women—for the men they date. This is because doing so would eliminate many, if not most, African-American males from their dating pools. Also, many African-American women are resistant to stepping outside their comfort zone of only dating African-American men.

African-American women and their children suffer because of this refusal to set minimal, universal standards. They also suffer from resistance to stepping outside an all-Black social comfort zone. There's no need for me to recite the statistics showing there is a numerical imbalance between the numbers of eligible African-American women and African-American men. You know there aren't enough eligible African-American men available to meet African-American women's marriage needs. You also know that this imbalance is exacerbated by the fact that African-American men don't restrict their dating and marriage options to Black women.

You know all of this and instead of taking the logical step of following Black men's example by also expanding your dating options, you lower your standards to accommodate an ever-dwin-dling and increasingly toxic pool of substandard African-American males. You engage in dumpster diving by dating and having children with Black male ex-convicts, unemployed individuals, playboys, and serial baby daddies.

You *and* your children suffer greatly because of your refusal to expand your dating and marriage pool to include quality men of all races and ethnicities.

Ladies, if you're serious about maximizing your odds of finding a quality man for a healthy marriage, then you'll expand your dat-ing pool to include quality men from *all* ethnic and racial groups. If you're serious, you'll also screen out mentally weak men, and seek out quality men who have a mind-set of self-efficacy.

CHAPTER 16

YET ANOTHER EMERGING, DISASTROUS TREND: NORMALIZING SINGLE ADOPTION AS 'PLAN B' FOR BLACK WOMEN WHO HAVEN'T MARRIED BY THIRTY-FIVE

Author and blogger Roslyn Hardy Holcomb sums it up in her recent post: http://roslynholcomb.wordpress.com/2009/07/07/just_say_next/ She's being very diplomatic about all of this. Let me mention some additional reality-check observations I've made while working in the court system:

1. Regardless of the mother's race, the *vast* majority of the children in foster care are Black men's children. Let's call these Black biological fathers "Ray-Ray" here.
2. Ray-Ray's *cast-off* or *had-to-be-taken-away* children often have negative genetic inheritances that include things like low IQs, developmental delays, and a predisposition to mental illness.
3. When Ray-Ray impregnates a higher-caliber Becky or Lupe, these women are more likely to *quickly* unload their unwanted half-Black children onto the child welfare system.

These children are usually quickly snapped up by infertile White couples, often at the urging of White social workers. These are usually *not* the children "left over" that are available to be adopted by single Black women.

4. When Ray-Ray impregnates a Reject Becky or Reject Lupe, these women are more likely to keep their half-Black children. These are the children that later have to be taken away from these women due to child abuse and neglect. If the particular Ray-Ray that fathered the child wasn't shacking in the abusive home with Reject Becky or Lupe, there was typically another Black male (let's call him "DeShawn") living in the abusive home with Reject Becky or Reject Lupe. Remember, these women are often rejected by men from their own groups after they have lessened their value (even more) by openly hooking up with Ray-Ray. **All of this means that the ultimately *had-to-be-taken-away* child has been subjected and exposed to all sorts of aberrant behavior. This context has grave implications for how the child will behave when later adopted by the often naive, single Black female parent.**

5. When Ray-Ray impregnates a Sheniqua, these Sheniquas typically keep their babies even when they know they can't properly take care of them. This means that they don't give them up for adoption as infants. The children have to be taken away from them when they're older. **Again, all of this means that the ultimately *had-to-be-taken-away* child has been subjected and exposed to all sorts of aberrant behavior. This context has grave implications for how the child will behave when later adopted by the often naive, single Black female parent.**

6. I have seen cases where the *had-to-be-taken-away* child was originally sexually abused by Ray-Ray or DeShawn, and placed in the home of unaware, unsuspecting, naive adoptive parents. **Some of these previously sexually**

abused, *had-to-be-taken-away* children then went on to molest the adoptive parents' biological children, or children in the new neighborhood. People need to understand that social workers don't always know the full extent of the child's past history. In some instances they know, but don't tell these sorts of things to prospective adoptive parents.

7. Many of the children who've been involved in the child welfare system become "system wise." In other words, they learn how to work the child-welfare system to threaten and manipulate their caregivers (natural parents, foster parents, guardians). God help the caregiver who attempts to set house rules for children *after* they've been in foster care for an extended amount of time.

I've heard recordings of some of these children (even small ones) threatening their caregivers with: *"If you don't let me do X (stay up all night, stay out all night, etc.)"* or *"If you make me do Y (homework, chores, etc.)" "then I'll call the social worker on you."* (And say that the caregiver hit them. Or that the caregiver touched their privates.)

The smaller ones learn this from the constant barrage of caseworkers and child-welfare attorneys repeatedly asking them, *"Does so-and-so hit you? Does so-and-so touch you in bad places?"* Many of these people ask these sorts of loaded questions, instead of asking open-ended questions (and following up on the child's response). The situation is unfortunate and corrupting.

8. I'll be blunt. Any woman who plans to use single-parent adoption as a Plan B to not finding a suitable husband needs to think carefully through all of these possibilities. I'm not trying to discourage single Black women from adoption, as long as they are making fully informed choices. It's understandable that folks don't want to miss out on

being a parent. However, the reality check is that it may be better for such women to explore the additional options of purchasing an infant from overseas.

Best of all would be for Black women who are in their child-bearing years to focus their attention and efforts on expanding their dating pool to increase the odds of finding a suitable husband. This means considering men from all races and ethnicities.

To have an entire generation of single African-American women *planning* on adopting Ray-Ray's *cast-off* or *had-to-be-taken-away* children as Plan B is an absolute catastrophe on many, many levels. It's a catastrophe that will ultimately help entrench the emerging *endless night of permanent underclass status for African-Americans*.

CHAPTER 17

AN OPEN LETTER TO AFRICAN-AMERICAN WOMEN WHO PUBLICLY STATE THAT THEY WOULD NEVER DATE OR MARRY OUTSIDE THEIR RACE

I've been thinking about the various ways that many African-American women unintentionally damage our collective image. All of which operates to our collective detriment as African-American women. One example is for an African-American woman to make loud, public pronouncements that she would never date or marry outside the race. This is usually said to emphasize the point that she would never date or marry a White man.

If you are an African-American woman who makes these sorts of public statements, I would ask you to consider the following questions.

Why do you feel the need to say this publicly?

Have you noticed that African-American women are *alone* on this planet in making these sorts of public statements?

You are alone in terms of race in saying these things. African-American men don't make these sorts of statements. Look at the numbers of African-American male artists who choose non-Black women as the romantic leads in their music videos. African-American men also don't restrict their dating and marriage options based on race. Look at African-American men's higher rates of interracial dating, mating, and marriage.

Why are you publicly narrowing your dating and marriage options when African-American men aren't doing this?

Similar to African-American men, women from other ethnic groups also keep their dating and marriage options open. This includes other women of color. No other ethnic group of women on this planet makes public statements that narrow their marriage options. African women don't make these sorts of public statements. Latina women don't make these sorts of statements. Neither do Asian nor South Asian women.

Even those women whose men are actively at war with Western White men, such as Arab women, don't make these sorts of public statements. If Arab women don't do this, why in the world are you doing this? Keep in mind the Arab woman is not making these statements even while her Arab man is busy following through on his hostility toward Western White nations. Unlike loud-talking, fake-militant Black men, deranged Arab men are running around killing their perceived White male enemies. And yet, the Arab woman *still* keeps her collective marriage options as open as possible.

African-American women are the only people on this planet that run around publicly saying they won't date or marry outside the race. The fact that nobody else is doing this should be a clue to you that this is not a good idea.

When you publicly talk about how you would never date or marry outside the race, you are inadvertently slitting our collective throats as African-American women. You are slitting our throats because you are inadvertently working to narrow our collective options. Why continue to do this?

How does publicly saying these sorts of things benefit you? I submit to you that it doesn't benefit you to say these things in public. There's no benefit or need for you to tell others that you won't date or marry outside your race. People catch the hint by your actions.

It also doesn't benefit other African-American women for you to make these sorts of public statements. Please stop making these sorts of public statements. These statements don't benefit you; meanwhile they harm the interests of the rest of your sisters and daughters.

Peace, blessings, and solidarity.

CHAPTER 18

DON'T MISS OUT ON MARRIAGE BECAUSE YOU'RE FIGHTING A CULTURAL WAR THAT BLACK MEN ABANDONED OVER FORTY YEARS AGO

I've had occasion to talk to African-American women who make public statements declaring that they would never date or marry outside their race. I'm always fascinated by some of the unexamined assumptions that seem to underpin these statements.

One assumption is the notion that African-American men and African-American women are involved in some shared struggle to uplift the so-called Black community. This is obviously untrue. It's also obvious that Black men abandoned that particular ideology forty to forty-five years ago! A quick observation of their general behavior confirms this. When Black men "get theirs," they are gone from the so-called Black community! Without a trace. And nobody questions this. Black women are the only ones encouraged and required to keep talking about rebuilding the now-dead Black community.

The second unexamined assumption is the notion that *"White people are our primary oppressors and enemies,"* and therefore "we must fight them." Somehow, many African-American women fail to notice that this idea never stopped African-American men from dating, having sex with, and marrying White women.

Any Black woman who believes this needs to rethink this idea.

First, the violent Black underclass long ago seized the "We're going to destroy African-Americans" mantle from racist Whites. The vast majority of the physical destruction of African-Americans is coming from other Blacks. The vast majority of the mental destruction of African-Americans (by means of anti-life hip-hop and other artifacts of Black underclass culture) is coming from other Blacks.

This earlier ideology has most of us ignoring this widespread destruction coming from other African-Americans. This ideology has us characterizing the internal demons that rob, rape, and murder other Blacks as "brothers" and "sisters." Instead of adequately protecting ourselves from these internal monsters, we focus on acting in whatever way we perceive is in opposition to whatever Whites are doing—even when what Whites are doing is healthy and productive. This defiant stance is the origin of the acting-Black madness. It's profoundly childish and self-destructive.

Second, we need to look at what Latinos are doing to us in places like Los Angeles (shooting down random Blacks, including small children, on the streets and driving Blacks out of certain neighborhoods by violence). We also need to look at what Latinos are doing to us in Florida (applying rampant employment discrimination against African-Americans). If we pay attention, we can clearly see that anti-Black, racist Latinos (which includes those Black Latinos who hate African-Americans) are second only to the Black underclass in being mortal enemies to African-Americans. We ignore this fact (to our peril) because of our obsolete "White people are our primary oppressors and enemies" ideology.

If we did a current ranking of who's racking up the most hate-fueled kills of African-Americans, we'd have to rank our mortal enemies as:

- African-American males in first place
- Latino males (of all races) in second place
- White males as distant, third-place contestants

Acknowledging any of this would require us to look at people's actions, and do some critical thinking. Most of us prefer to deal in slogans and assumptions. Assumptions like the notion that *"other (foreign) Blacks and people of color are automatically our friends and allies."*

Ladies, remember that you are *alone* in letting anything (including ideology) narrow your personal choices. African-American men have never narrowed their dating or marriage choices to support ideology. Please consider the following partial list of individuals before you do so. (It has to be a partial list, because a full one would probably take up this entire book.) Also, pay attention to whether any of the "Black love" champions you know ever comment about these men. Do they only start talking about Black love when it looks like you might expand *your* dating options?

Amiri Baraka, Charles Barkley, Harry Belafonte, Billy Blanks, Julian Bond, Taye Diggs, Father Divine, Frederick Douglass, Julius Erving (Dr. J), Frantz Fanon, Marvin Gaye, Cuba Gooding, Jr., Gregory Hines, Rick James, James Earl Jones, Quincy Jones, Van Jones, Reginald Lewis, Thurgood Marshall, Major Owens, Sidney Poitier, Adam Clayton Powell, Prince, Richard Pryor, Lou Rawls, Lionel Richie, Dennis Rodman, Seal, Russell Simmons, O.J. Simpson, Wesley Snipes, Clarence Thomas, Melvin Van Peebles, Ben Vereen, Herschel Walker, Walter White, John Edgar Wideman, Billy Dee Williams, Montel Williams.

CHAPTER 19

WHAT YOUR DAUGHTER CAN EXPECT IF SHE ATTENDS A HISTORICALLY BLACK COLLEGE, OR EXCLUSIVELY DATES BLACK MEN WHILE ATTENDING A PREDOMINANTLY WHITE COLLEGE

In an earlier post, I focused on the literally life-threatening trends that are emerging at historically Black colleges and universities. Basically, these places are becoming epicenters of HIV/AIDS infections. I've been focused on the literal life-and-death consequences for young Black women of attending historically Black colleges and universities.

Now, let's also consider the emotional damage that African-American female students suffer by attending historically Black colleges and universities. The same social dynamics that are creating HIV/AIDS spikes at these colleges also inflict a lot of emotional suffering on those Black female students who manage to avoid contracting HIV/AIDS.

During the earlier conversation, a couple of readers described in detail what current-day college life is like for: (1) African-American female students at historically Black colleges and universities, and (2) African-American female students at predominantly White colleges who restrict themselves to only dating Black males. It's not a pretty picture (my comments are in italics):

A reader named KM said: "...Honestly, the same problem is going on at PWIs (I attended one), it's just greater at HBCUs. I went to a BCS football school and the percentage of Black students was close to 5 percent of the total student population and the female/male ratio was 60-40. (Mind you, the overall female/male ratio was 46-54 in favor of men.)

"So, if you wanted to date in the BC (which I didn't because even though I didn't know of the BWE *[Khadija speaking: BWE = Black women's empowerment]* blogs back then, I *did* know who was asking me out on real dates (WM) and I chose that over being asked out to hook up (BM)), and once you took out the out gay men, there were three women to one man. Then the men who were already dating out, that reduced the number to four to one.

"So women were competing to see who could do splits, hang on the ceiling fan, anything to keep a Black man. People who would tell me that they wouldn't ever have sex without a condom but then would be pregnant within months because they didn't insist on one because they wanted to keep their man. Threesomes, getting trains ran on, etc. only to get that HIV test and show up HIV+. Knowing full well who were on the DL but still having sex with them. Then even though it was a rural school, there was still a remnant of the Black criminal element that managed to find their way up there (only to get arrested sooner rather than later because the police up there didn't play) and some BW got entangled with them.

"BW are playing Russian roulette with their sexual lives and their health (physical and mental). If any of you have female daughters about to go to college, *PLEASE* educate them because no matter where you go now, it's real and these dangers are out there. And I'm doing my part by talking with the young ladies I know from church and at work about what is going on. Knowledge is power."

A reader named E said: "I wholeheartedly agree that Black women need to consider the social climate before choosing a college. I attended a big rural state school in the Northeast, about 10 percent Black. Most of the Black students were from big cities (Hartford, New Haven, Bridgeport) and had attended big-city high schools. They were usually very uncomfortable in the rural college town and clustered at the African American cultural center and Black events.

"There was much policing of authentic Black behavior, but of course more so for women. Even at college, Black folks frowned at me for my music, my dress, my opinions, my 'untamed,' unrelaxed hair, and my dating choices and I *did not* care. I had come from private school and a suburb and I was used to being among Whites and middle-class folks and socialized as I always had with whomever I found stuff in common with.

"I also very much noticed that Black men would date Latinas and go to their parties but Black girls never dated Latino guys. We also had a great, nationally ranked bball team with all the issues that come along with prominent Black male athletes dating whoever they want (as they can and should) and Black women having hurt feelings and trying to get and keep them by doing sexual Olympics. I had a gorgeous friend have a man tell her she was 'too dark' for him to bring home. She was so, so hurt.

"But yes, imbalanced gender ratios and Black women's refusal or fear to date out keep men with too much power. And you know the adage, absolute power corrupts absolutely. There was man-sharing on campus and some of these men acted a fool. And at least a few of the city girls got pregnant and had babies. I remembered being so confused as to why anyone would go to college just to get knocked up by Tyrone from back home. But that was what they knew and being in college didn't seem to change that.

"I dated two different White guys in college, both for about a year and a half each, with plenty of dating for fun in between. I am pretty sure had I not dated those two guys, I would have had no boyfriends in college.

"I know plenty of Black girls who never had any dates at all for FOUR years. (Khadija speaking: Oh, my God.) It was so sad. On Friday nights, the White girls would go out, the 'exotic' girls would go out, and usually the typical-looking Black girls would stay in and eat popcorn and watch movies and relax their hair. I like movies and popcorn, too, but I didn't go to college to recreate the all-girls' sleepovers of my childhood. (Khadija: Still shaking my head in sorrow—these young ladies missed so much by clinging to 'nuthin' but a BM')

"I actually considered a PWI women's college, Smith in Mass., but decided I wanted a social life that included seeing males on a daily basis. Some of the Black girls in my dorm would quietly pull me aside and ask where they could meet a cute White guy who "liked Black girls." I'd say 'Ooh girl, the library, the dining hall, and class.'

"I am cute, but not that cute. I was just friendly and open, I expressed my interest subtly so the guy knew I wouldn't laugh in his face and say 'Naw, I don't date nothin' White.' Seriously, the Black women who do that ruin it for everybody! (Khadija: As I noted in an earlier post about this, no other ethnic group of women says things like this. No other women of color say things like this—including African women. African-American women need to stop cutting their own throats with these sorts of unnecessary statements.) Even my White friends would ask where I met my guys. I always played dumb with them. Hahaha."

Ladies, is *this* what you want for your daughters?

CHAPTER 20

WHY IT'S IMPORTANT TO HAVE DATING EXPERIENCES IN COLLEGE

We've recently had several discussions about the dangers and structural difficulties faced by young African-American women at historically Black colleges. We've also talked about the difficulties faced by young African-American female students who limit themselves to dating only Black men while at predominantly White institutions.

When I bring up these issues during in-person conversations, there are always several adult African-American women who minimize the importance of this issue by saying that these young women need to focus on their studies and not on dating. I believe that young ladies should focus on both.

Focusing only on one's studies and not gaining experience in positively socializing with the opposite gender sets young African-American women up to have difficulties later in life. In short, they're missing the opportunity to develop many important relationship skills. These skills are needed to navigate the world of dating in a way that increases the odds of marriage. This topic is extremely important and deserves its own separate discussion.

The Readers' Money Quotes are statements that are of such

insight and importance that they merit frequent and loud repetition. These examples come from two astute readers named Lisa99 and TertiaryAnna. First, my comments:

In an original post, I said that I'm also concerned about the young (and not so young) AA women who are making all sorts of dating errors simply from lack of experience. This is why I was so outdone by the comment from the individual who was cheerleading HBCUs—that she made good friends and got a great career because of attending an HBCU. As if that's all there should be to college. Well, it's not!

Getting experience in positively socializing with the opposite sex (for those who are straight) is a critical part of the normal college experience. It's an important part of transitioning into adult life. Women who go through college without a sufficient amount of dating experiences are setting themselves up for difficulties in their adult lives.

I never thought about this until somebody explicitly mentioned it to me (since this is so far removed from my experiences in college), but it must be a real hardship for a woman to start learning about how to act on real dates when she's twenty-three, twenty-five, thirty, or older.

That "just keep your legs closed" talk is a nice slogan, but what does that really mean for a woman whose first sexual experience is after age thirty-five? I had never considered the problems that so-called mature virgins have until somebody brought this to my attention. (Let me clarify that I'm not talking about the sex itself, the mechanics of which are fairly simple and easy to learn, I'm talking about negotiating the reciprocity issues surrounding the sex.)

Being a grown woman who's trying to figure out real dating and sex for the first time is not a good position to be in. To my way of thinking, part of the value of college is having a convenient forum to work through those sorts of experiences, so that you're ready for committed, adult relationships and marriage by the time you graduate.

I think about one of my colleagues who's over thirty years old. I had to explain to her why the one guy who had taken her out on a real date was offended and irritated by her action of pulling out her purse when the waiter brought the bill.

At first, she didn't understand how she had lowered herself in his eyes. She didn't understand that this one action let him know the low treatment that she was used to. It also let him know the low caliber of Negroes that she had seen before him. Negroes who want to go dutch. Negroes who want and expect a woman to pay for the expenses involved in the date.

Not to mention that the (Black) man was offended (as I explained to her and he later *told* her) by her assumption that *he* was anything like the shiftless Negroes she was used to seeing.

After talking to her at length, I realized that much of this was the result of a lack of actual dating experience (as opposed to hook-up experiences). This lack of actual dating experience matters. A lot.

In response, Lisa99 said: "I'm noticing this more as well, as I speak with my peers in their early thirties. While I might not have been the earliest bloomer, I did start dating and going out more by my final year of college and it made it so much easier for me to navigate the world of dating and relationships once I left school.

"It's sad to me to see thirty-something women asking for certain basic advice about going on dates. They almost have no idea what to do, and I have encountered a lot more mature virgins than I've expected. They wake up one day and realize that while they've been told to wait for marriage, but how can they get married if they haven't even dated? And no one seems all that interested in giving them assistance in the dating arena. They just pat them on the back for keeping their legs closed. (*Khadija speaking: Exactly. And this is the reason why I'm irritated with all the smug recitations of the 'just keep your legs closed' slogan. Keeping one's legs closed still leaves a lot of problems unaddressed.*)

"I also had a friend who did the same thing with reaching for a bill to pay. It wasn't because of bad experiences in the past with DBRs who wanted to go dutch, but she felt that she needed to "prove" to this man that she didn't want anything from him. (Khadija speaking: *That's absolutely insane. And it's yet another example of how African-American women buying into DBRBM— Damaged Beyond Repair Black Men's—propaganda, as in 'I gotta prove that I'm not a so-called golddigger,' sets them up for failure when they encounter real men who behave like normal men.*)

"I told her in advance of the date that she shouldn't do this, but she did anyway, and she said he looked very shocked by it.

"They did not go out on another date. There were other things she did on the date that didn't play in her favor, but that was probably the kicker.

"If she had more dating experience, she might have been able to understand why the man was bothered by her actions."

In reply to another reader, I said, Yes, during college, one is in training for learning how to manage a balanced life. This training involves how to properly handle one's business regarding grown-up pleasures, including but not limited to:

1. How to drink alcohol socially without ever getting drunk; how to stick like glue to your female friends if you're going to get drunk; and how to reduce the risks of making yourself vulnerable to being slipped date-rape drugs. (Friends and I eventually learned to order bottled water to reduce some of these risks.)

2. If you're a woman who wants to be sexually active, how to have sex without developing a reputation. (Which involves a lot of planning and calculation. Which involves learning how to carefully screen guys. It also involves learning *"not to piss where you have to eat."* In other words, if you're going to have casual sex be sure to have it only with men who are far removed from your normal social circles. This also means men who are not friends with any of the guys you would want to actually date.)

Another reader said, "...*From what I could see, they weren't* *learning anything from these experiences (I assume this because they kept making the same mistakes over and over again). I'd take being a 'mature virgin' any day over that."*

In reply to this comment, Tertiaryanna said, "This is a false dichotomy. There are other options besides 'bad experiences vs. no experiences.' Bad choices can be labeled as negative without having to compare them to anything, and should be avoided when possible.

"But the topics of what makes positive male-female interactions and when is the optimal time to learn them are separate issues.

"It's important to realize 'mature virgin' here isn't really the issue of sexual inexperience. It's the fact that a person in their mid-thirties hasn't had the kind of romantic interactions that are typical for a person their age. If one wants to be celibate then that's one thing.

"But when a person makes a 'choice' from lack of options, then it's really not a choice at all. So singledom can be seen in a different light for these women who are told not to look for mates, or that they're going to find them in spite of a steadily dwindling pool, or keeping them so busy in their churches that they're taken out of the dating realm by default, by undermining their efforts at personal advancement by keeping them as the de facto family watershed, or by having their chances of marriage materially reduced by telling them that 'pretty bad' is 'good enough.' These women do want to be coupled, and when there aren't personal reasons why they are not, then it's important to look at structural reasons.

"Using that last sentence as a starting point, their decisions may be less of a choice than the reflection that their options have been narrowed by attitudes and people who don't really have their best interests at heart.

"Clearly, this isn't a universal statement: people have different reasons and choices to make. Some people choose celibacy or singledom and it in no way lessens anything about them.

"But the issue here is to ask what factors in a social or religious environment lead its members to atypical results when those results were *unwanted*.

"For the US, the national average age of marriage is twenty-five to twenty-seven years. A conservative estimate is that people dated for a year before getting engaged and were engaged for a year before the wedding. So the average age to meet one's spouse is shifted down to twenty-three to twenty-five. Also, assume that the first person that one dates does not become that person's spouse. So in the years between eighteen and twenty-three, a person is learning what they want in a relationship, how to advocate for themselves, and how to develop their own quality traits for marriage.

"It doesn't mean people get it perfectly done, because there's a high divorce rate that could possibly be contrasted to the never-married rate. But when a group of people is doing at thirty-plus what their peers are doing at twenty-plus, then there's something that needs to be carefully examined. (*Khadija speaking: Exactly. This is a serious problem. When African-American women structurally limit their chances of gaining dating experience in college by: (1) attending historically Black colleges—where there are huge gender imbalances (meaning many fewer Black male students), or (2) by only dating Black men while they're attending PWIs, then they set themselves up to be years behind their peers in learning vital relationship skills. For just one example, it's better for a woman to make, and learn from, the previously mentioned 'reaching for the bill mistake' at age nineteen than at age thirty-three!*)

"The sex part is trivial. It's the lack of dating experience (when that experience was desired) that's the problem. Because when a twenty-two-year-old doesn't know how to advocate for herself, then part of that is just the age. But when a normal woman in her full adult maturity has difficulty or inexperience navigating these same issues, then it's valid to ask what circumstances got her to that point."

TertiaryAnna said all of this much more clearly and elegantly than I could. Lisa99 and TertiaryAnna, thank you for providing these Readers' Money Quotes!

Addendum: My sisters, please remember: You were robbed of your birthright!

It is your *birthright* as women to have reasonable opportunities for legitimate, wholesome marriage and family life. You were robbed of this by narrowed options and circumstances. These circumstances are the result of African-Americans buying into corrupt dogma.

There is no need for you to feel embarrassment, shame, or a feeling of stupidity. There's no shame in being robbed. You were robbed.

There's no need to blame yourself. Most people accept—without questioning—whatever is considered normal in their immediate circles. If nobody explicitly warned you about any of this, how would you know?

As TertiaryAnna said, "I think that some people are invested in making sure that BW don't get warned. I think this is why the feelings of shame and embarrassment are common: deception works best when the target feels responsible for the cheat. It reduces suspicion on the cheater and makes their job much easier. So if a BW is exposed to people who want to advance their own agendas by using her resources, they will encourage her to focus on her own actions while discouraging her from looking at theirs."

Ladies, there's still time for you to claim your birthright. But you can't look back. You can't succumb to regrets or self-blame. What's done is done. Be happy you have the health and resilience to be able to reach for your birthright. Don't look back at Sodom. You have to keep looking and moving forward into better circumstances. Into the Promised Land.

CHAPTER 21

BLACK WOMEN: WHY DO YOU LET 'BECKY, LUPE, J. LO., FATIMA AND MEI LING' INDIRECTLY PIMP YOU?

I'm going to say some things the plain and rough way here.

I don't care if African-American men choose non-Black women (also known as "Becky, Lupe, J Lo, Fatima, and Mei Ling") as wives. I don't care if, like so many Black male celebrities and other prominent Black men, they give practically all their personal worldly goods to these non-Black women and their non-Black in-laws. That's the great thing about freedom. We're all free to do as we please.

I don't care if Becky and other non-Black women take these Black men for all they are worth, like Michael Strahan's White ex-wife. "Becky and the girls" often feel that they need to get all they can get from any man, including Black men. Unlike many African-American women, they have no confusion about expecting men to protect and provide well for them and their children. And I notice that nobody begrudges these non-Black women for getting all that they can get. I don't begrudge them either. None of this is my concern.

My issue is this: African-American women, why are *you* subsidizing Becky and these other women? I'm wondering what's wrong with *you*.

What's wrong with some of you? Don't you understand that when you support a Black male who's hooked up to Becky and other non-Black women, you're also subsidizing Becky, Lupe, J Lo, Fatima, and Mei Ling? In some cases, you are using your *hard-earned-from-working-a-job money* to subsidize a life of leisure for these women. She's getting a pedicure and a massage while you're beating the streets going to a job.

What's wrong with some of you, that you let another woman indirectly pimp you? Tyrone can give all the money and resources he wants to give to these women—he just needs to get these resources from *somebody other than me!* When you give something to Tyrone—so he can give it to Becky, Lupe, J Lo, Fatima, and Mei Ling—you are actually giving to Becky, Lupe, J Lo, Fatima, and Mei Ling. She's living large on *your* dime. Why don't some of you understand this? What's wrong with you?

I don't care where Becky and the girls get their sustenance from, as long as it's *not* coming from *me*. It's not in my interests to subsidize non-Black women and *their* children. If my resources are ultimately going to be used to support a woman, then I want that woman to be African-American like me.

Some of you are silly enough to call yourself "enlightened" in that you don't care that Tyrone is using the resources you give him to support Becky and the girls. I say that you're a fool. Your behavior is out of step with basic, human norms for heterosexual women. Most heterosexual women are not going to subsidize unrelated, female strangers from other ethnic groups.

I'm highlighting heterosexual women because there's nothing in this setup that is of any possible interest to most straight women. They're not getting romantic thrills and chills in exchange for subsidizing these other women. They're not getting sexual gratification in exchange for supporting these other women. They're not getting material benefits in exchange for supporting them.

Foolish straight women will allow men to pimp them in the hopes of gaining at least one of the above-mentioned benefits. But for most straight women, the idea of being pimped *by another woman* is out of the question. That's the breaking point for most straight women. But this apparently is not a breaking point for many African-American women. Some of you think it's praiseworthy for you to subsidize Black men's non-Black wives.

Your behavior is out of step with how women from every other ethnic group on this planet behave. Non-Black women have no interest in subsidizing you and your Black children. Let me give you a simple, everyday example. Non-Black women generally won't buy diapers that have a Black baby on the package. The diaper companies know this, which is why they avoid having infant Black models on their packages.

Don't call them racist for this. It's simply a natural, self-protective instinct that women from every other ethnic group have. They have the natural, self-protective instinct to want to keep their resources as in-house as possible. These other women know that when their resources stay within their ethnic or racial group, there's a higher chance of these resources eventually flowing back to their own children. Everybody understands this. Everybody—except indoctrinated African-American female zombies.

Some of you are giving to Tyrone—so he can give to Becky, Lupe, J Lo, Fatima, and Mei Ling—while *you* and *your* children are suffering. What's wrong with you?

Let's be clear. This is not about Black men's romantic choices. I don't care about Black men's interracial relationships and marriages. Now, I do want Black men to stop their hypocritical efforts at blocking Black women from following their example in expanding their marriage options. More importantly, I want African-American women to stop wasting their support on people who don't support them.

This is about the stupidity of African-American women rallying around O.J. Simpson. The same Mr. Simpson, if I remember correctly, who cheated on his Black wife with a White woman. The same Mr. Simpson who divorced his Black wife to marry the White woman. Mr. Simpson, who hadn't said the word "Black" since he married his White ex-wife. Mr. Simpson, who went back to chasing after White women exclusively after the acquittal in his criminal case (by a jury that had some Black female jurors, if I remember correctly).

This is about the stupidity of African-American women rallying around Prof. Henry Louis "Skip" Gates. Skip Gates who was fixated only on the White male police officer involved. Not on the Black male police officer who was also involved in his arrest. And not on the White female neighbor who had originally called the police on him. Skip Gates, who wanted to send flowers to her. Skip Gates, whose White wife had said nothing publicly on his behalf. Some African-American women are still foolishly upset on behalf of Skip Gates.

This is about the stupidity of African-American women rallying around Van Jones. His White wife also hasn't bothered to speak out publicly on his behalf.

Since the established pattern is that these non-Black wives won't bother to speak out for *their own Black husbands when their husbands are under attack*, what do you think they'll do for you and your Black children? Meanwhile, some of you are still screaming in support of these women's husbands.

You haven't figured out that many African-American men are assigning you a lesser status based on their inner belief in White supremacy. This means that for many African-American males, when it comes to choosing a woman to protect and provide for, they select non-Black women to pamper.

But when these same Black men get in trouble and need somebody to do some heavy lifting on their behalf, then they look to you. You cooperate with this workhorse status when you run to rescue these men. All the while, their non-Black wives sit back, relax, and refrain from lifting a finger to rescue their own Black husbands.

This idiotic behavior of supporting people who don't support them is a large part of why Black women and their Black children are suffering.

CHAPTER 22

THE MASS 'GASLIGHTING' OF AFRICAN-AMERICAN WOMEN

"Gaslighting" is a term that's derived from the scenario of the stage play *Gas Light,* and the two movies titled *Gaslight* that were adapted from the play. The plot involves a scheming husband who tries to drive his innocent, young wife insane. He does this by insisting that what she sees is not real, and that she's imagining things.

A recent book by therapist Dr. Robin Stern, *The Gaslight Effect,* describes gaslighting behavior as a form of emotional abuse.

My Sisters, Stop Putting Up With Being Gaslighted

As I browse the Black blogosphere, I see conversation after conversation where African-American women acquiesce to Black men's lies. I see *nonstop* intrusions where Black men invade Black women's blogs and Black women's conversations, and try to browbeat Black women into denying the reality that's all around them.

Some of you surrender to this. Some of you start to doubt what you've seen with your own eyes, and what you've heard with your own ears. Some of you start second-guessing reality to try to appease African-American males.

For one example, some of you start to soft-peddle the colorism that Black men inflict on Black women. So, you pull out the same, tired, few names of Denzel Washington and Samuel Jackson as shining examples of Black male celebrities that married darker-skinned women. As if that's representative of what Black men do when they get money or prominence. So, you pretend that you didn't hear what Ne-Yo said (*"all the good-looking kids are light-skinned"*) or what Yung Berg said (*"I don't date dark butts"*) or what:

Amiri Baraka, Charles Barkley, Harry Belafonte, Billy Blanks, Julian Bond, Bill Cosby, Taye Diggs, Father Divine, Frederick Douglass, Julius Erving (Dr. J), Frantz Fanon, Marvin Gaye, Cuba Gooding, Jr., Gregory Hines, Rick James, James Earl Jones, Quincy Jones, Van Jones, Reginald Lewis, Thurgood Marshall, Steve McNair, Major Owens, Sidney Poitier, Adam Clayton Powell, Prince, Richard Pryor, Lou Rawls, Lionel Richie, Dennis Rodman, Seal, Russell Simmons, O.J. Simpson, Wesley Snipes, Clarence Thomas, Melvin Van Peebles, Ben Vereen, Herschel Walker, Walter White, John Edgar Wideman, Billy Dee Williams, Montel Williams and too many other Black men to name (the list would take up this entire book) did.

For another example, some of you soft-peddle the frequency and amount of violence that African-American men commit against African-American women and girls. Or you pretend that women from other ethnic groups are being attacked and killed with the same frequency as African-American women and girls. No, they're not. You already know that in your heart.

I used to refer to this *"You didn't see what you saw; you didn't hear what you heard"* scam from Black men as "playing the nut role" or running the "Jedi Mind Trick." But I recently realized that it's much more sinister than any of that.

It occurred to me that the low- and no-value Black men who engage in gaslighting actually want African-American women to ignore that there's a campaign in progress to destroy our minds, spirits, and lives. This gaslighting is intended to be to the death. To your death!

My Sisters, Stop Taking Relationship Advice from Black Men

Stop taking relationship advice from Black men. It should be obvious to you that they don't have your best interests at heart. The reality is that many Black men work to break your spirit under the guise of giving you relationship advice.

Stop listening to their advice. Stop listening to Black men's nonstop spirit-breaking campaign of verbal abuse against Black women. By their collective behavior, most African-American men have made it clear that they are unable and unwilling to function as legitimate husbands, or as protectors and providers for Black women and children. The statistics on Black male paternal abandonment of Black children, the overwhelming African-American out-of-wedlock birthrate, and the lack of marriage among African-Americans are a testament to this fact.

Instead of speaking the truth about their mass failure to function as protectors and providers for African-American women and children, most Black men blame Black women for their ongoing failure to do what non-Black men do for their women and children. Instead of speaking the truth, many Black men work to break African-American women's spirits. Often, it's done under the guise of giving you relationship advice.

It's time for more African-American women to reject Black men's soul-killing messages of "You're too Black and dark and therefore ugly" or "you're too picky" or "you need to lower your standards and give a brother a chance" or "don't nobody want you anyway." (Incidentally, the same Black men who demand that Black women lower their standards are the same men who hypocritically mock those Black women who have illegitimate babies by low-quality Black men. Haven't you figured it out? You can't win by listening to these men.)

The first reason African-American women need to reject that "Don't nobody want you anyway" message is the simple fact that it's simply not true. There are non-Black men (and Black men from other ethnic groups) in this country and in the global village who *can* and *do* appreciate African-American women's beauty, resilience, and high spirits. There are men from other ethnic and racial groups who would be able, willing, and eager to protect and provide for individual African-American women as legitimate husbands and fathers. All any woman needs is to find *one* such man.

Most African-American women have had the experience of being respectfully approached by non-Black men. Most African-American women reject these respectful advances out of a misguided sense of racial loyalty—a sense of racial loyalty that is not reciprocated by Black men. Black men date and marry whomever they please, irrespective of race or ethnicity. It's long past time for African-American women to do the same. Any African-American woman who is serious about marriage needs to expand her dating pool to include quality men from all racial and ethnic groups in the global village.

Stop listening to Black men's lies and double standards in criticizing Black women. Overall, African-Americans' double standards are rooted in racial self-hatred. The negativity and hatred that many African-American men spew about African-American women is one such double standard. It's a scam that's designed to keep Black women trapped in a losing pattern of trying to appease Black men who can't be appeased.

Don't be deceived by this scam. The sheer physical numbers don't support the notion that listening to Black men's soul-killing messages to Black women is of any productive use. Even if all African-American women decided to twist themselves into pretzels to appease Black men's dishonest complaints, there simply aren't enough Black men to go around. There aren't enough African-American men to provide enough husbands for those Black women who foolishly restrict their dating pool to Black men. The physical numbers aren't there even before screening out the African-American men who are violent, convicts, drug addicts, or gay.

Black men's bad-faith critiques of Black women are similar to the double standards that some African-American consumers have for Black-owned businesses. Many Black men will marry obese, "trailer park" non-Black women but also demand that Black women be polished and near-flawless "diamonds." This is exactly parallel to the way African-American consumers will shop in filthy and rude Arab and Korean-owned stores, while simultaneously demanding that Black-owned businesses look and act like the jewelers at Cartier.

I prefer that more Black-owned businesses have the highest standards, but quality and service are not what's motivating African-American consumers' choices. If it was about quality and service, then African-Americans wouldn't flock to these filthy and rude Arab and Korean-owned stores. The real motivation is rooted in a lack of racial self-respect, and a burning desire to be validated by non-Black others.

In a similar fashion, Black men's actions demonstrate that their true motives are the same with this issue. Black women have eyes to see what many Black men actually do. We see the obese, uncouth, and overall uncivilized non-Black women that so many Black men gleefully take up with. We notice that many of them have the same traits that these men accuse Black women of having.

If African-American men were sincere in their complaints about African-American women, then so many of them wouldn't chase after and marry non-Black women that have the same negative traits that they accuse Black women of having.

Stop listening to Black men's insincere "I believe in Black love" and "interracial marriage is genocide" double-talk. This rhetoric is a scam. Black men only start talking that "Black love" rhetoric when Black women start talking about following Black men's example of doing whatever works for them, including expanding their marriage pool to include non-Blacks. You won't hear Black men engaging in this Black love rhetoric when other Black men are chasing and marrying non-Black women. They reserve those lies for Black women's ears. This is because African-American men benefit from the status quo.

African-American men want to keep African-American women available as a surplus, booty-call supply of lonely, desperate, single women. When African-American women are happily married, then they are not available to be exploited by African-American men. This is the true motive underlying the deceptive Black love sloganeering from Black men: To keep African-American women tricked, trapped, and available to be exploited.

Walk Away from Anybody Who Tries to Gaslight You

This mass gaslighting of African-American women only happens because most of us cooperate with it. If you want to survive (much less thrive) you'll stop acting as if you have to prove reality to Black men or the Black-male-identified women who parrot their lies. Reality is similar to gravity in that it doesn't require *anybody's* approval to exist (with the exception of God's).

When somebody tells you the bleeding, gaping wound *that they inflicted on you* does not exist, you need to get away from that individual. You certainly need to stop listening to him and his lies.

CHAPTER 23

TRUE FELLOWSHIP: BREAKING BREAD

The Barriers to True Fellowship among Black Women

We know what's wrong. We talked about the barriers to true fellowship during an earlier conversation.

Busy with Their Lives

We discussed how many Black women are busy with their lives. We described how this often translates into many Black women depending on their husband or boyfriend for all of their emotional needs. The problem with such an arrangement becomes obvious when there is a divorce or separation. These are often the same women who only have time for friends when they are between relationships with men.

- Will you commit to becoming slightly less busy with your life?
- Will you commit to making time to pursue true fellowship with other Black women?

Modern Gadgets Provide Pseudo-Contact

We discussed how gadgets like the telephone, e-mail, and

instant messaging only give the illusion of keeping in touch with people. We noted how these gadgets make it easy to lose contact with friends for years without even realizing it. We recognized that deep relationships are based on shared experiences. If we're not physically spending time with one another, then we're not building shared experiences.

- Will you commit to turning away from the gadgets as much as possible?
- Will you commit to seeking out in-person contact with your sister-friends?
- Sometimes personal contact is not possible, and the best substitute is a phone call. On these occasions, will you commit to following up that phone call with a handwritten note? Sent by snail mail?

The Prevalence of Selfishness

We talked about how prevalent selfish, self-absorbed behaviors are among Black women. We noted how too few Black women are willing to compromise to spend time with a friend. As an example, we considered the question of how many of us are willing to go see a movie that we are not thrilled about that our friend wants to see. We noted that very few Black women are willing to inconvenience themselves in any way to spend time with a friend. Very few Black women are willing to interact with other women in any way that is not to their total liking and at their complete convenience. We noted how most Black women will only go the extra mile for men.

Craziest of all, we noted how even lonely Black women engage in these same selfish and self-absorbed behaviors. We recognized that besides Black women who won't reciprocate fellowship, there are other Black women who genuinely can't reciprocate fellowship. These are usually the pack mules among us who don't want to work on solving their problems. They're the Black women who are only looking for a way to function while leaving their problems firmly in place and deeply entrenched. And they're the Black women who want to use your fellowship to help them shoulder burdens that they have no business carrying.

- Will you commit to sifting through, and stepping around, large numbers of user-type Black women to find the few gems that are among us?
- Will you commit to sidestepping Black women who can't reciprocate your fellowship?

There Is No Quick Fix

We recognize there is no quick fix to these barriers. We know that fellowship isn't built overnight. We know that it's also not built while operating on autopilot. It's built choice by choice. Action by action.

- Will you commit to taking deliberate and sustained actions in support of building fellowship?

Building Fellowship by Breaking Bread

Regular shared meals are a large part of what binds people together. It has been this way from the beginning of human life. This is why all religious traditions have practices that involve large, communal meals. It's frightening to consider how disconnected many (most?) Black people have become from this primal, *human* connection to one another. In many Black homes, family members take their plates and eat separately with each member sitting in front of a different television. Some of us go for weeks and even months without once actually sitting together and sharing a meal with another human being. This is profoundly unhealthy. In fact, it's anti-human. In the long run, it's anti-survival. Even so-called primitive people knew that isolation equals death.

Until the last two generations or so, most Black folks understood this too. Our everyday lives and routines as a people reflected this basic wisdom. We ate dinner together as a family every evening. Dinner was served at a predictable, consistent hour. We went to Big Mama's home for Sunday dinner. We were connected to one another by regular, shared meals that continued for *years*.

At some point, our connections to one another began to come apart. We became "busy with our lives." Dinner was frequently, and then regularly, eaten on the run. Then dinner started being eaten separately by various family members. We began to keep dinner warm with the conscious, deliberate intention of family members regularly coming late to the dinner table. Finally, we started immediately putting portions of a freshly cooked dinner in the refrigerator. We did this with the conscious, deliberate plan of family members eating hours apart from one another.

Over the years, we gradually became "too busy" to go over to Big Mama's house for Sunday dinner. By the time Big Mama passed away, we only shared these sorts of large, communal meals at Thanksgiving. But even Thanksgiving dinner was frequently eaten while sitting in front of the television.

We have now reached a point where many of us only share these sorts of large, communal meals at funeral repasts. If we're going to turn this situation around, we have to model the behavior that we want to see take root among our people. If we want true fellowship, we have to engage in regular and sustained efforts to build it. Choice by choice. Action by action. One shared meal at a time.

- Will you commit to breaking bread with friends regularly?
- Will you commit to sharing a meal (preferably dinner) once a week with friends?
- At a minimum, will you commit to not allowing more than ten days to go by without breaking bread with a friend?

PART IV: THE SOJOURNER'S PASSPORT TO EFFECTIVE ACTIVISM

CHAPTER 24

AN OPEN LETTER TO PRINCETON THEOLOGICAL SEMINARY

11/26/08

Nancy Lammers Gross – Dean of Student Life

Iain R. Torrance – President

I am writing to express my outrage over the fact that Dr. Yolanda Pierce, an esteemed scholar and professor at your seminary, was attacked in a racist flier distributed by students at your campus.

It was an act in support of a vile, racist, hate campaign for these students to distribute this flier under the virtual Ku Klux Klan hood of anonymity.

It is an act of institutional racism for the Princeton Theological Seminary to continue its failure to properly address this orchestrated hate campaign against one of its own professors.

Furthermore, the Seminary's failure thus far to properly address this campaign is also an abomination. Especially for an institution that purports to prepare its students "to serve Jesus

Christ in ministries marked by faith, integrity, scholarship, competence, compassion, and joy, equipping them for leadership worldwide in congregations and the larger church, in classrooms and the academy, and in the public arena." [Princeton Theological Seminary Mission Statement]

If proven, engaging in such a hate campaign is surely conduct that should provide the basis for disciplinary action such as suspension or dismissal. Reasonable minds that are untainted by racism recognize that accountability requires much more than silently accepting a few weak, insincere apologies for an outrage of this magnitude.

I am strongly urging the Seminary to follow its own procedures and hold a hearing pursuant to the process described in Section 6.6 of the academic regulations contained within The Princeton Seminary Handbook. [Academic Regulations, Section 6.6: "Procedures Associated with Other Causes," The Princeton Seminary Handbook]

The Seminary needs to follow its own regulations, hold full hearings regarding all of the students involved, and make a decision regarding these students' continued relationship to the Seminary, irrespective of their ethnic or racial backgrounds. This is only fair.

A failure to follow your own regulations would make it abundantly clear that Princeton Theological Seminary has truly lost its way. If the Seminary is unwilling to follow its own rules by conducting a full hearing, I and as many others as I can persuade to join me, will pursue every avenue available to make the public at large, the media, the Seminary's financial supporters, and the entire world aware of the Seminary's depraved indifference toward the racist denigration of Black academics. My outrage is shared by each new person who learns of the Seminary's inaction. There will be accountability.

Note to Readers

Apparently, racist students at the Princeton Theological Seminary recently distributed a flier attacking a Black professor named Dr. Yolanda Pierce. Dr. Pierce is an Associate Professor of African-American Religion and Literature at the seminary. This situation has been described by a Black professor at Princeton University, Dr. Melissa Harris-Lacewell, in one of her blog posts. http://princetonprofs.blogspot.com/2008/11/i-am-having-drink-join-me-if-you-like.html

Another blogger has made a call for us to come forward and express our displeasure with this example of yet another attack on Black women. I have sent the above letter in response to this call. **Silence in response to these sorts of attacks endangers us all.** Allowing these sorts of attacks to pass in silence endangers those of us who work in academia. It endangers those of us who are currently students in these institutions. It endangers those Black girls who will grow up to follow our footsteps to attend or work in these institutions.

Without seeing the flier itself, my conscience won't allow me to demand a specific outcome to holding a disciplinary hearing. **However, I don't have to see the flier itself, or know all the intimate details of this situation, to insist that Princeton Theological Seminary follow its own rules and regulations.** I am not saying that others are incorrect in calling for the students' suspension or dismissal without having seen the flier. I am simply stating what I feel is appropriate for *me*.

I know there will be critiques of this call to respond in the absence of the flier. I know that for some of us, the urge to respond will decrease if we learn there was a Black student involved in distributing this material. Let me point out a few real-world aspects to these sorts of situations.

First, people tend to lawyer up fairly quickly in these situations. Everybody knows there is a real possibility of litigation resulting

from this. At which point, people will be skittish about further dis-
seminating this material. For any purpose. This also means that
there's not going to be much public discussion (if any at all) of this
from those who are directly involved.

Second, it doesn't matter if it turns out the racists were able to
find a Black-woman-hating Black male student to participate in
this outrage. It doesn't matter if it turns out that they were able to
find a self-hating Black female student to participate. This is what
sophisticated racists do—they look for "colored" accomplices as
a back-up alibi in case they get caught. They do this so they can
falsely claim, "See, it wasn't racist. A Black guy helped with this." **It
doesn't matter. Everybody involved should be held accountable for their actions, irrespective of their ethnicity or race.**

Third, I am willing to give one of my sisters who is a respected educator the benefit of the doubt. If someone of Dr. Melissa
Harris-Lacewell's stature (Associate Professor of Politics and
African American Studies at Princeton University) is publicly stating
that a Black female colleague was personally attacked in a racist
flier distributed on campus, I'm going to give Dr. Harris-Lacewell
the benefit of the doubt that something that merits a response
occurred.

Finally, those of us who are sincerely interested in protecting
Black women from attacks will look for, and find, creative ways to
respond to these situations while still honoring our own criteria for
response. As I noted above, I won't demand a specific outcome
without seeing the flier for myself, but I can and will demand that
Princeton Theological Seminary follow its own rules, and treat this
situation with the seriousness that it deserves.

CHAPTER 25

TABLE TALK FOR ACTIVISTS, PART 1: SUPPORT PRINCIPLES, NOT INDIVIDUALS

We now have several generations of African-Americans who have never come up through, or experienced for themselves, the discipline of an actual social movement. Most of us have only seen social activism from the perspective of an outsider watching a television soundbite from some "big man" spokesperson or leader. Most of us have never seen the nuts and bolts of social activism. Nor have most of us made any real effort to study what happened with our predecessors in any great detail. I can see the negative effects of these deficits in some of the cyber-activism that I've witnessed over the past year or so.

One negative effect is that we are often reinventing wheels. Another result is that we are being deceived and duped by the same anti-justice strategies that were in operation during the 1950s and 1960s.

Yet another effect is the general failure to think these matters through to the detriment of whatever efforts we are pursuing. I am not any sort of expert on activism. However, I was blessed to have participated in the anti-apartheid struggle when I was in college. Looking at what's going on now, I realize just how precious that experience was. For all the above reasons, I feel the need to share what little experience I have. I feel the need for us to talk about some things related to activism.

To that end, let's have an ongoing series of "table talks" about the nuts and bolts of activism. Starting with *Strategy No. 1: Support Principles, Not Individuals*.

Modern African-Americans are not the same type of people as our ancestors. We can see that just in comparing how resourceful our ancestors were versus how helpless we've learned to be. This fact has implications for activism. Aspiring activists need to recognize that modern Black victims of atrocities are not the same as past atrocity victims.

Modern Black victims of an atrocity will often behave in ways that are not helpful, and are *contrary*, to the cause of justice. The modern victim is often not looking for justice to be served. Instead, they are looking to be rewarded for their silence, or they are looking to hide within their silence. Either way, their actions make it that much harder for justice to be served. For examples of this, consider R. Kelly's many, many victims. Including the victim that was the subject of his recent criminal trial.

This means that activists need to make some decisions up front. What is more important in a particular situation? Catering to the victim's desire to get paid for their silence? Catering to the victim's desire to hide within silence? Or is there a greater collective interest that takes priority?

With the sexual-predator situation, I believe there is a greater collective interest in getting a sexual predator off the streets—no matter *what* his past victims want. It is more important to me to prevent any more Black girls from being victimized in the future. As far as I'm concerned, his past victims don't get to decide that it's OK for the rest of our young Black girls to remain in danger because he's on the loose.

This has to be a case-by-case analysis. With each situation, we must weigh whether what any particular victim wants is endangering the rest of us. And we have to ask ourselves whether we are willing to run that risk to accommodate the victim's wishes.

The bottom line is that many modern Black atrocity victims have wishes that are contrary to justice, and contrary to our collective interests. They will often do things that burn the people who supported them. This is why we must support principles, and not individuals.

CHAPTER 26

TABLE TALK FOR ACTIVISTS, PART 2: MAKE THE OPPONENT FOLLOW THEIR OWN RULES

One of the rules for power that Saul Alinsky discussed in his book, *Rules for Radicals,* was the strategy of making an opponent follow their own rules. This is sound advice for several reasons that I discussed in a comment to the post, *"An Open Letter to Princeton Theological Seminary."* Here is the comment in full:

"With my 'editorial' comments about all of this, I wanted to give the general audience an example of an inside view of 'lawyer think' that they can apply to situations.

"My first step in evaluating any situation (or preparing a cross-examination of a witness) is to compare what the person did/is doing to what they're supposed to be doing.

"Almost every institution and profession has rules, regulations, and codes of conduct that are supposed to govern people's conduct in various situations. Universities, government offices, etc., typically have their own internal rules and regulations. Each profession has its own ethical code of conduct that is established by leading organizations within that profession (ABA, AMA, etc.).

"So, with a university situation, my first step is to look at the student handbook to see what sorts of things are (or should be) covered by disciplinary rules. The next step is to look at the disciplinary rules themselves. This gives an objective guide for evaluating a university's response to an outrage...

"...Comparing their actions to their own rules and codes of conduct also prevents activists from being confused by defensive, bad-faith whining from racists about how 'we sponsored a "healing and learning" festival. What else do you people want from us?!'

"I don't want some fake 'healing and learning' festival. As a first step, I want PTS to follow its own rules & regulations (hold disciplinary hearings concerning all of the students involved)."

Please know that most of the handbooks, internal regulations, etc., that I've seen are fairly straightforward. You don't have to be an expert to understand them.

I believe that part of the reason why some activists are easily tricked by their opponents' stalling tactics such as insincere calls for dialogue and healing festivals is because they haven't researched the rules that are supposed to govern how an institution handles a particular situation.

Insisting that, at *minimum*, an opponent follow their own rules strengthens an activist's position.

First, because it's hard for opponents to make deviating from their own rules sound reasonable. Second, most institutions' in-house attorneys will warn key players that deviating from known standards creates heightened exposure to lawsuits.

Finally, insisting that an opponent follow its own rules applies mental pressure to whatever semi-decent and decent people exist within the opponent organization. Most people like to have a self-image of being reasonable and fair. People like to have this self-image even when it's not accurate. Most people also like to believe the organizations that they serve are legitimate institutions. Not crime cartels.

Take the time to research whatever rules govern the situation you're mobilizing around. Knowing the applicable rules can only strengthen your activism.

CHAPTER 27

TABLE TALK FOR ACTIVISTS, PART 3: DON'T DELEGITIMIZE YOUR STRUGGLE BY MAKING 'WHITE PEOPLE ARE DOING IT TOO' ARGUMENTS

Whenever the topic of wrongs committed by Blacks comes up, there are always plenty of Black folks who link and measure our evil deeds with those of Whites. I believe that this traditional, knee-jerk response is a serious error. As much as we like to scream about how we're being victimized, many of us feel perfectly comfortable victimizing others.

The *"White people are doing it too,"* or *"White people did it worse,"* or *"White people are doing it more"* arguments are totally irrelevant when considering the evil of some of our people's actions. Furthermore, these arguments are ethically repugnant; and even worse, a dangerous strategic liability for African-Americans' long-term interests.

Ever since the *Princeton Theological Seminary* post, White, racist trolls from PTS have been stalking several Black activist blogs. This blog is one of them. It pleases me to know that these racists are still smarting from this blog's (and other blogs') call for justice regarding the hate crime at PTS.

I had a brief exchange with one of the racist PTS trolls in the comment section of the "Negative National Security Impact of Damaged Beyond Repair Black Men (DBRBM)" post. This particular racist said:

"In all fairness to Black guys, White guys are the original DBR. We just didn't just go rape some people. We colonized a bunch of people, wiped out some civilizations and started a couple of world wars. Black men have a loooooooong way to go to match that. And really, who do Muslims hate more than evil, White, European guys?"

I responded: "Anonymous: Hmmm. You could be a DBRBM pretending to write in as a WM. (No, your anonymous note doesn't have quite the right tone for that.) Or your primary issue could be that you're an anti-Muslim bigot of any ethnicity. (No, that doesn't sound quite right either.) Or, you could be one of the Princeton Theological Seminary (PTS) racists who is still smarting from this blog's, and other blogs', call for justice at PTS. DING! DING! DING! By George, I think that's it! Funny how you're still stalking activist Black blogs.

"Whatever. (Yawn.) It really doesn't matter. Ayatullah Murtaza Mutahhari gave a concise summary of the Islamic position in his book, Social and Historical Change: An Islamic Perspective. Since Islam is oriented toward justice, those who benefit from this orientation are those people who are oppressed. Those who lose are those people who are oppressors. Muslims have a problem with whoever it is that's doing something wrong. Remember that, Anonymous. With justice in mind."

As the exchange continued, the racist troll was eager to try to elicit a "White people have done it worse" response from me. You may wonder why would a White racist want to hear a Black person agree with that argument. Answer: Because these sorts of arguments almost always serve his (racist) interests! In many different ways.

Making 'White People Are Doing It Too' Types of Arguments Serves to Delegitimize Your Struggle

White racists *like* to hear that sort of reasoning and arguments from Black folks. The racists like it because these type of arguments serve to delegitimize our struggles for justice!

The "White folks are doing it too" arguments let everyone know the speaker is not interested in justice. It lets everyone know the speaker is not taking a stand based on principle, but instead based on ethnic favoritism of some sort.

Engaging in these arguments plays into White racists' public relations strategy of characterizing our struggles as corrupt hustles and shakedowns.

When you make these sorts of arguments, you are helping to convince neutral, non-Black bystanders that your cause is unworthy of their support. Here's why: Unless you have worked to establish an ACLU-type reputation for advocating for the U.S. Constitution *across the board*, it looks as if you simply want any and all Black criminals to go unpunished when you make these sorts of statements. It looks like you are callously disregarding the pain that Black predators have inflicted on other people. It looks like you have no ethical center to your arguments. It looks like you have no concern for public safety. *Finally, it looks like you have no common sense.*

Non-Blacks have no inherent interest in having Black predators go unpunished.

Those audience members who remember some of the other comments from the White racist PTS trolls will recall that these racists *assumed* that we would not want a Black hate-crime perpetrator punished. They assumed that our calls for justice were calls for ethnic favoritism.

Over the years, you've heard some of the racists' pet phrases: "special treatment" and "special interests." You feed into this characterization by making "White people are doing it too" arguments. Please know that it seriously throws White racists off their game when you demand justice across the board.

White Racists Have Nothing to Lose by Admitting Their People's Past Crimes

First, you should realize that the entire topic is a joke to a racist troll. He knows that his collective will not be held accountable for their history of genocide and slavery. So he can make all the historical admissions he wants, without it undermining *his* people's interests. The additional joke for him is that he's dishonestly pretending to shed crocodile tears for *long dead* victims of color, while ignoring and brushing off the suffering of *still-living* victims of color.

Your Struggle Has a Lot to Lose by Making These Arguments

When we join the racist troll (and others) in making such arguments, we are undermining our people's interests. We are furthering the racist characterization of our struggles as ethnic favoritism-based hustles.

We are also driving away potential non-Black allies. You see, the only thing that non-Blacks usually hear from us are demands that Black criminals escape punishment. As well as a steady stream of excuses and denials of the evil done by some Blacks. They almost never hear any of us calling for any Black predator to be punished.

Second, keep in mind that racists do not wish you and other Black people well. They do not want to see the African-American collective cleanse itself of the crime and evil within. Racists are comfortable when Black folks excuse and enable evils that these same racists would never tolerate running rampant within *their* collective.

"White people are doing it too" arguments serve to excuse and enable evil. These sorts of arguments also undermine our long-term interests. It's long past time to stop using them.

CHAPTER **28**

TABLE TALK FOR ACTIVISTS, PART 4: HANDLING 'INTERNET IKE TURNERS'

If you are a Black woman blog host who supports Black women and girls, you have to be prepared to handle the Internet Ike Turners that are guaranteed to show up at your site. (Head scarf flutter in salute to Gina McCauley, blog host of *What About Our Daughters* for coining the phrase "Internet Ike Turners.")

Internet Ike Turners are Black men who are enraged at the idea that *any* Black woman, *anywhere*, is thinking about *any* issue in terms of Black women's interests. You see, Internet Ike Turners are determined to maintain the current status quo of Black interests being defined solely as whatever benefits Black men, *period*.

Internet Ike Turners (IITs) euphemistically refer to this status quo of Black male empowerment *at the expense of* Black women and children as "Black Unity." And they will attack any forum that questions or challenges this status quo.

If you use your blog to question this status quo, then they will attack *you*. They will also seek to disrupt your blog discussions.

Recognizing Common IIT Tactics

The first step to handling this online aggression is to recognize it for what it is: an attack. Too many Black women bloggers mis-read this behavior as legitimate dissent and discussion. That's not what the behavior is about at all. It's about derailing, and shutting down, any discussion that might raise Black women's conscious-ness. I'll focus on the IITs' favorite attack techniques, but please take the time to read the entire linked article called *"25 Tactics for Truth Suppression"* here: http://www.benfrank.net/disinfo This article covers the full range of disruptive tactics.

Play Indignant

Avoid discussing any of the points that are raised, and instead talk about how offended you are by the very premise of the discus-sion. Naive opponents will discuss and debate the merits of your decision to take offense at the discussion.

Hit and Run

Leave a short, sarcastic comment and then run off before anyone can respond. An alternative is to return to leave other comments while *ignoring* other participants' responses to your original comment. Naive opponents will continue to respond to you, instead of moving the discussion forward without you.

Straw Man

Misrepresent your opponent's argument into something that's weaker and easier for you to rebut. Spend all of your comments responding to this fake, straw man argument, and not to anything your opponent actually said.

Deny Reality

Act and speak as if the real, negative circumstances facing African-American women don't exist. Act and speak as if the African-American collective is a paradise filled with stable, loving, married households. Act and speak as if the masses of Black men are protecting and providing for Black women and children. In short, deny reality. Imitate the posture of 1950s Southern racists who just *knew* that "their darkies" had every reason to be happy living under segregation, and *would be* happy if it wasn't for "outside Communist agitators." Naive opponents will start discussing and debating the existence of your alternate reality, instead of the original issue at hand

Invoke Invented or Skewed Statistics to Deny Reality

This is a variation of the above technique. Naive opponents will start discussing and debating the merits of your fake statistics, instead of the original issue at hand.

Start a Flame War

Say something insulting or condescending to goad opponents into emotional responses. This way you can shift the conversation away from the issue at hand, and onto other people's emotionalism. For extra-credit points, leave a link in your insulting comment to an IIT blog to lure opponents there to be insulted some more.

Change the Subject

This tactic is usually used in combination with at least one of the other tactics listed. It's also the ultimate goal of all the earlier tactics.

Stay on Point: Stop Holding Town Hall Meetings for Internet Ike Turners

The first error that many Black women bloggers make is not recognizing these disruptive tactics for what they are: attacks. The second error many women bloggers make is entertaining this nonsense.

If you are an activist blog host, please understand that it is inappropriate to allow oppressors to use your blog to advance their agenda! You don't owe your oppressor equal time. Would you allow the Klan to use your blog forum to spread their message? Well, the Internet Ike Turners are the same as the Klan. I think that sometimes we forget this.

As a blog host, unless you have the skills to use the IITs' comments as teachable moments, you probably should not publish their comments. By arguing with IITs, you are allowing them to redirect the discussion away from the original point, and away from your discussion goals. For audience members, the most productive response is usually to ignore the Internet Ike Turners' provocations, and stay focused on moving the discussion forward.

CHAPTER 29

TABLE TALK FOR ACTIVISTS, PART 5: HANDLING 'IKETTES'

As well as having a strategy for handling attacks from Internet Ike Turners, activist Black women blog hosts need to consider how they will handle destructive behavior by Black women.

I divide these destructive Black women commenters into three broad (sometimes overlapping) categories: Ikettes, backbiters, and fools. This post will focus on Ikettes. Ikettes are Black women who actively support Internet Ike Turners. By Ikette, I specifically mean a Black woman who goes to Internet Ike Turner blogs to demean and degrade other Black women bloggers. *That* behavior is what it takes for me to consider somebody an Ikette.

Before I go any further, let me stress that I'm not trying to dictate what other activist bloggers should do about the Ikettes (as I've defined them above). My concern (as with the other *"Table Talk for Activists"* posts) is that many folks don't seem to have thought any of this through at all.

For example, I see several (presumably activist) Black women bloggers that have individuals I consider to be Ikettes in their blogrolls. When I see that, I wonder if it occurred to these women that perhaps it would be a good idea to try to screen folks before placing them on their blogroll. I wonder if it occurred to them to keep their eyes and ears open for what folks are doing on *other* blogs before lending them the credibility of being listed on their own blogs.

Again, my concerns are for activist Black women's blogs. Here's why this matters for activists:

You never know what campaign you might feel compelled to support or lead with your blog in the future. Don't assume that your blog is, or will always be, insignificant. For all you know, you could find yourself dealing with an issue of the *utmost* importance to Black women and girls such as the Dunbar Village Atrocity .

If you have a cadre of *unknown* and *unidentified* Ikettes who have insinuated themselves into your blog home in positions of trust, you have enabled their Internet Ike Turner masters to use them to sabotage your blog campaign!

It's one thing if you are aware of these Ikettes and have *knowingly* allowed them to participate at your blog, for whatever reasons you might have. Again, I'm not trying to tell other people what to do with their blogs. The *knowing, informed* choice to allow an Ikette to participate is one thing. It's a totally different situation if it hasn't even occurred to you to scrutinize the people hanging around your blog home.

As far as I'm concerned, this lack of scrutiny is negligence. Nobody required you to take on the mantle and the responsibilities of being an activist. That was your choice. The oppressed and aggrieved people who might be counting on your blog campaigns deserve better than that. The rape victim that you're seeking justice for deserves better than that. The molestation victim that you're seeking justice for deserves better than that. The hate-crime victim that you're seeking justice for deserves better than that.

The pursuit of justice requires more than that. The pursuit of justice requires that you do due diligence, and act proactively.

CHAPTER 30

TABLE TALK FOR ACTIVISTS, PART 6: BACKBITING AND OTHER DESTRUCTIVE FORMS OF DISAGREEMENT

Backbiting Is Usually The Result Of Mishandling A Disagreement

Upon reflection, I realized that backbiting is usually the result of the backbiter mishandling disagreement. It begins when the backbiter discovers that she's unable to get the other person to agree with her. The backbiter then starts going to various *other* venues to disparage the person who disagreed with them. I've watched this happen repeatedly with commenters on various blogs.

Here's the typical sequence of events for this:

The commenter is unable to get the blogger to agree with her. The commenter then tries to flip the script, and claim the blogger that they are backbiting is intolerant of dissent. From the incidents that I silently observed before I even started my own blog, that's not these backbiters' true issue at all. Their real issue is that they were unable to get the blogger to change their position. And instead of graciously agreeing to disagree, they skulk off to other forums to whine about how the blogger would not change their position to agree with them.

This is dysfunctional and destructive behavior. Let's talk about the constructive management of disagreements.

Recognize that Most Disagreements Will Be Managed, Not Resolved

As Frank Hecker stated in his essay *"Handling Disagreements in Open Collaborative Projects,"* most disagreements will be managed, not resolved. For Black women's empowerment blogs, the point (as I see it) is to work together to pursue our broader, shared goals. The point is not to convert other discussion participants to every single tenet of our personal beliefs.

Recognize the Difference between Critical and Noncritical Points of Disagreement

To work together to pursue broader, shared goals we actually have to *have* shared goals. Trying to work with people who do not share one's goals automatically leads to infighting. Even if a group of people has shared goals, they also need to have shared core *values* to be able to cooperate enough to get work done. Trying to work with people who do not share one's core values automatically leads to infighting.

For example, I believe in economic empowerment for Black women. However, I would not be able to cooperate with persons who feel that it is appropriate for Black women to seek this empowerment through the sex trade.

The problem with how many of us handle disagreement is that we inflate every point of disagreement into a false core value. Through our emotions, we turn every point of disagreement into a dealbreaker. Whether or not the disagreement is over an actual core value, we need to learn to walk gracefully away from disagreements.

Gracefully Walk Away from the Disagreement

People create much unnecessary friction and strife when they refuse to walk gracefully away from a disagreement. Instead of agreeing to disagree and moving on, they do destructive things. Sometimes they run to other venues to backbite the person who disagreed with them. Backbiting is when the target of the verbal attack isn't present to respond.

As well as backbiting, there's another destructive behavior that I call "the running battle." This is where the combatants openly rehash and refight their battles with each other over and over at a never-ending series of venues. As a result, the strife that was originally contained within one setting is spread to multiple settings.

Another destructive behavior that people sometimes engage in is to stay and fight with the person who disagreed with them. There are two main stay-and-fight techniques that I often see. The first is to rehash needlessly the original point of disagreement. It's one thing to state one's full position on an issue when it naturally comes up in discussion (including a point of disagreement). It's something else to drag the point of disagreement into unrelated conversations.

The other technique is to insist on having the last word in a disagreement. I see this a lot with commenters on blogs, which always amazes me. It would never occur to me to expect to have the last word about a topic in *somebody else's* house. Especially if the person I'm disagreeing with is the blog host!

On this blog, I will at times allow dissenting readers to have the last word in a disagreement. I try to be a gracious host. However, I won't do that if I feel the point of disagreement is critical. Also, people need to understand that they are not entitled to have the last word in *somebody else's* house. That's a courtesy that might be extended, not a requirement.

Gracefully walking away should be the general practice whether the disagreement is about a dealbreaker issue or not. If it is, engaging in destructive behavior (such as backbiting and staying to fight) will likely create an extra, unnecessary enemy. If the disagreement is about a nonessential matter, engaging in destructive behavior will make it difficult (if not impossible) to cooperate with that person in pursuit of broader, shared goals.

Over the last century, many Muslim reformers such as Hassan al-Banna (the founder of the Muslim Brotherhood) have recognized the important organizing principle that activists should cooperate on the issues they agree on. And that they should excuse one another on the issues they differ on. I believe that this is good advice.

CHAPTER 31

TABLE TALK FOR ACTIVISTS, PART 7: AN OPEN LETTER TO BLACK WOMEN BLOGGERS, YOUTUBERS, AND EVENT ORGANIZERS

I've already discussed the public handling of Internet Ike Turners in an earlier post. Now, because of subsequent events, I feel the need to mention some behind-the-scenes precautions that women who have an online presence need to take. Here's a comment that I made in response to one of Faith's recent posts (she's the blog host of *Acts of Faith In Love And Life*, which is on my sidebar blogroll).

"Well, first things first: I believe that every woman blog host and YouTuber needs to take security issues seriously. I remember reading a news story awhile back about how women blog hosts across the board (and no matter how innocuous their subject matter) are so much more likely to be blog stalked and harassed by male readers.

"Meanwhile, so many women (especially AA women) have been programmed to nervously laugh off male acts of aggression. For example, I'm thinking of a disgruntled BF reader at my blog who was angry when I made a comment about this awhile back.

"She characterized my comments as paranoid and defiantly stated that she was not going to 'live in fear,' etc. In other words, she was not going to take online security issues seriously, nor was she going to take Damaged Beyond Repair Black male (DBRBM) commenters' online aggression seriously. She took this posture even though the hate comments from DBRBM had driven her off her own blog! Even though she shut down her own blog due to BM harassment, she angrily ran to another BW's blog to badmouth me because I talked about security issues. The mind boggles.

"All of this was before a young Black woman named Asia McGowan was murdered by a DBRBM who was spewing hatred toward BW on YouTube. He was spewing hatred in response to her innocuous YouTube videos. (Incidentally, there's a BM website that hails this killer as a hero. I'm not going to name it. I don't give publicity to racist, violent, sexist sites.)

"In any event, I strongly urge all women blog hosts to:

"(1) Keep track of the trolls' IP addresses and geographical locations;

"(2) Maintain a log of print outs of the trolls' comments (whether you publish them on your blog or not, you need to keep a file on these nuts);

"(3) And most importantly, be prepared to call your local FBI field office, local law enforcement, and local law enforcement in the troll's jurisdiction *the moment* the troll submits a comment that you feel is in any way threatening!

"In terms of this latest DBR-killer, it just goes to show that despite the seeming differences between various types of nuts (racists, DBRBM, sexists, religious fanatics, etc.), what they all have in common is that they hate women. Peace, blessings and solidarity."

Ladies, an Internet Ike Turner has already killed a young African-American woman. He wasn't the only IIT that's capable of, and eager to commit, violence against women. There are others. Many others.

While browsing through various blogs, I can see that many of the African-American women commenting online haven't really let this sink in. There is still hesitation in their voices about calling law enforcement on those Internet Ike Turners that make threats. It's as if you don't want to acknowledge that many of these nuts would like to harm you physically.

Many of you want to minimize the threat by pretending that it's all about a particular Internet Ike Turner's mental illness. And yes, from what readers have sent me of their ramblings, several of them are clearly mentally ill. But in focusing on any particular Ike's probable mental illness, you're missing the main point. The main point is that the Internet Ike Turners are threats. Threats to be managed by proper security precautions and techniques. To a woman—like Asia McGowan—who is wounded, maimed, or killed by an Internet Ike Turner, does it matter if they're mentally ill? No, it doesn't.

A secondary point that many women want to fixate on is that mentally ill Ikes are encouraged and supported by a viciously sexist African-American subculture that supports violence against Black women and girls. Modern African-American culture supports, encourages, and excuses all sorts of violence against Black women and girls—from the sexual molestation of Black girls that R. Kelley's Black fans support, to the beating of women that Chris Brown's Black fans loudly support. Does any of this matter to a woman who is wounded, maimed, or killed by an Internet Ike Turner? No, it doesn't.

Ladies, focus on what matters! What matters is taking proper security precautions for your online and off-line activities. I would strongly urge you to take the steps I've outlined above for your online work.

For any off-line gatherings that you sponsor, I would strongly urge you to hire security. From what I've been told, several Internet Ike Turners are making online threats of physically disrupting future events sponsored by and for African-American women. You need to take these threats seriously and prepare for them.

As an additional step, I would urge event organizers to hire a private investigator to film and photograph every Black man who:

- Seeks entry into the event (since they have no legitimate reason for being there unless they are an invited speaker)
- Loiters around outside the event
- Appears to be watching who's going in and out of any event that you're sponsoring.

Some of the Internet Ike Turners might not be bold enough to crash your event; but some of them *will* want to conduct hostile surveillance on the Black women who attend. You need to watch the people who are watching *you*. This is what law enforcement agencies do by filming activists at protest marches.

Ladies, get real about your own safety and the safety of your guests.

PART V: THE SOJOURNER'S PASSPORT TO FULFILLING WORK

CHAPTER 32

WHY BLACK WOMEN SHOULD LEAVE THE HELPING PROFESSIONS

It's long past time for Black women to seek their bliss, and therefore stop getting involved in public service careers.

Black Public Service Is Mostly Balanced on Black Women's Backs

It's important for us to recognize that all the "helping" fields are balanced on Black women's backs within the Black collective. Black male professionals generally *don't* go into helping sorts of jobs or careers. They're generally not spending their work life trying to uplift downtrodden Black people. They're too busy pursuing their own bliss. Black women need to catch the hint and do likewise!

There are many reasons Black women need to walk away from public service.

Your Service Is Not Appreciated

First, Black women's efforts in the helping fields are not appreciated. Generations of African-American women have devoted their working lives to serving Blacks. And what did they get in return? Disrespect from the Black collective at large that they served, stress, and aggravation. And the pleasure of being made the scapegoats for mass African-American cultural failures. In fact, Blacks have made a tradition out of insulting the Black people who service their needs.

You Are Being Used as Scapegoats. Exhibit No. 1: The Public School System

Let's use the generally unappreciated, and disrespected legions of Black female public school educators as a case study.

Consider the disrespectful, dismissive attitudes that most Blacks have about public schoolteachers. Do these African-Americans even realize that the majority of countries on this planet don't have free public school systems? Judging from our loud whining, we don't know this basic fact that puts everything in perspective. In most countries, people have to buy school uniforms and books. They can't just dump their children off each morning with no further investment on their part. They can't simply use the schools as a free baby-sitting service. Which is how most African-Americans use the public schools.

The "Grassroots" Destroyed the Public Schools and Then Blamed You. Exhibit No. 2: Social Promotion

Are we willing to acknowledge the disastrous effects of some of the initiatives promoted by non-middle class, "grassroots" Black activists? No, that failure is usually swept under the rug, and Black professionals are scapegoated. Let's discuss one such fiasco from my hometown, Chicago. Years ago, local grassroots Black parent-activists browbeat the Chicago Board of Education into implementing a policy called "social promotion."

Social promotion is the practice of passing children onto the next grade even though they haven't mastered the material of their current grade. The grassroots parent-activists claimed that it was just too damaging to Black children's delicate psyches to flunk individuals who didn't master their grade-level material. Keep in mind, the grassroots pushed this initiative, not the Black middle-class parents who were given even more incentive to remove their children from the local public schools.

The Chicago Board of Education gave in to these demands and implemented social promotion. The same grassroots activists complained bitterly about the resulting increased exodus of middle class Black children from the neighborhood public schools. The result was years of children being passed onto the next grade even though they weren't prepared. After years of damage was done, some other grassroots activists started complaining that Black children were graduating from high school without knowing how to read.

Well, wasn't that the logical, predictable outcome of adopting the policy the "grassroots" Blacks said they wanted? The Chicago Public Schools have been struggling for years to undo the damage caused by listening to these activists.

The Black Underclass Stigmatized Their Own Children to Get Free 'Crazy Money.' They Then Blamed You for the Mass Drugging of Black Children. Exhibit No. 3: Supplemental Security Income (SSI) for Children with Disabilities

Grassroots Blacks also like to whine about the prescription drugging of Black children in the public schools. What these grass-roots individuals never acknowledge is that there was a fad among many Black welfare mothers to get some free "crazy money." They got this free money from having their children labeled (and stigmatized) as mentally retarded and emotionally disturbed.

The same way Black welfare recipients often migrate to states with better benefits, they also pay attention to opportunities to get increased payments.

Many Black welfare mothers were looking to get their children labeled as emotionally disturbed and mentally retarded to get their kids onto the SSI disability rolls. The point was to get more free money without having to work for it. If you know any social workers, ask them about the "crazy money" from SSI. Its formal name is *"Supplemental Security Income (SSI) payments for children with disabilities."*

From the SSI website:

"HOW DOES THE SSI DISABILITY PROGRAM WORK FOR A CHILD?

"To be eligible for SSI benefits, a child must be either blind or disabled. A child may be eligible for SSI disability benefits beginning as early as the date of birth; there is no minimum age requirement. A child may be eligible for SSI disability benefits until attainment of age 18 (see definition of disability for children).

"When the child turns age 18, we evaluate impairments based on the definition of disability for adults (see definition of disability for adults).

"A child with a visual impairment may be eligible for SSI blindness benefits if the impairment meets the definition of blindness (see the discussion of statutory blindness).

"WHAT ARE THE CRITERIA FOR A DISABLED OR A BLIND CHILD?

*"If under age 18, whether or not married or head of household, the child has a physical or **mental condition or conditions** that can be medically proven and which result in marked and severe functional limitations; and the condition(s) must have lasted or be expected to last at least 12 months or end in death; or if the child is blind, the same definition of blind applies as*

for adults." http://www.socialsecurity.gov/ssi/text-child-ussi. htm (emphasis added)

I wouldn't be surprised if SSI has tightened the eligibility requirements for the crazy money in the current economic climate. However, over the years many grassroots Black mothers signed up their children for this benefit when the gravy train was still running. And yet, so many Blacks want to blame the public schools (read: Black female teachers) for the numbers of Black children who are in special education classes, or are being drugged.

You Are Free to Leave This Madness and Disrespect Behind

Black women deserve to receive better than this in exchange for the use of our talents, skills, and hard work. It's time to go where our work will be appreciated and valued. The moral of this story is that it's time for Black women to stop going into helping professions and careers. African-American women need to:

- Stop teaching at the non-university level
- Stop participating in social work in any capacity
- Stop participating in anything at all that involves servicing the Black poor and underclass

It's time for Black women to seek our bliss just like everybody else.

CHAPTER 33

THE ART OF BLACK-OWNED BUSINESS: AVOID CUSTOMER RESISTANCE BY HAVING A COLORLESS BUSINESS

African-Americans who will survive and thrive through business creation need to understand that our business terrain is not the same as it is for other business owners. The material and physical terrain is the same, but potential customers' mental terrain is different when it comes to Black-owned businesses.

There are a series of mental barriers that most potential customers (especially Blacks) have against supporting any business activity controlled by Black people. We need to assess this resistance honestly, factor it into our business plans, and work around it. Too many African-American business owners assume that it's simply about offering high-quality products and services. It might be that way for non-Black businesses, but this is not the case for Black-owned businesses.

The reality is that non-Blacks don't want to give their economic support to Black-owned businesses. And neither do Black people!

With African-American consumers, this aversion to supporting Black-owned businesses is not about quality or service. If it were about quality and service, then these same Black consumers would not flock to shop in filthy, rude and potentially deadly Arab- and Korean-owned businesses. (Consider the murder of Latasha Harlins in a Korean-owned store in Los Angeles.)

The reality is that African-Americans don't and, for the most part, *won't* support a business if we know that it is Black-owned.

I always knew that if I wanted to start my own firm, I would need to hire a White attorney to pretend to be my partner, and to be the main public face of the firm. It is well known by other ethnic groups that African-Americans won't patronize Black professionals. Over the years, I've had several White (Jewish) colleagues approach me and offer to be the White front if I ever decided to start my own practice. (For a percentage of the fees, of course.)

I always knew that if I ever wanted to open a grocery store in the Black community, I would need to hire an Arab to be the front. Or, as my friends would tease me, I needed to wear hijab so my hair never showed, and try to pretend to be an Arab.

The successful Black businesses located in Black areas (that I'm aware of) tend to hide their true ownership. If the owner is working on the premises (such as with a gas station or laundromat), he pretends to be just an employee. This is the informal rule for operating a successful Black-owned business in Black America. The only exceptions to the rule are hair salons and barbershops.

Most African-Americans will only patronize a business if they think that it's *not* Black-owned.

The other route to success is to have a faceless business, such as selling e-books online. These sorts of businesses do not depend on Black support and are geared to get some of everybody's money. The bottom line in the US context is that most non-Blacks won't patronize a business if they know that it is Black-owned. And Blacks won't either.

The same behavior applies across the board. Black business owners generally won't hire Black accountants or lawyers. Black

THE ART OF BLACK-OWNED BUSINESS ❧

entertainers and sports figures won't hire Black agents, accountants, lawyers, or trainers.

I've seen several comical situations where the Black professional complaining that Blacks won't hire him also does not hire other Black professionals for *his* needs. A Black personal trainer that I hired years ago had this issue. He whined about how the Black football players he knew wouldn't hire him. Yet, he didn't hire any Black professionals either. He also had a fixation on White women, incidentally. He didn't like it when I told him that perhaps the football players "didn't see color" and felt that "people were people." (Which were the excuses he used for chasing after White women exclusively.) I never would have hired him if I had known all of this at the beginning.

Anyway, on those rare occasions when Blacks do hire Black attorneys, they don't want to pay. And Blacks like to come to Black lawyers with nonsense that we don't dare approach White lawyers with. Such as, *"Can I get a payment plan? Can I pay you in installments of $10 a week?"* White attorneys (quite reasonably) typically require huge chunks of money—as in thousands of dollars—upfront even to consider taking a case. Black clients will pay them (especially Jewish attorneys) without any hassles.

A few years ago, I overheard a Black woman trying to play a similar game with a local Black spa owner. She wanted to throw a spa party for her friends (translation: she wanted to show off), but didn't want to pay the full price. While waiting for my massage, I overheard the owner patiently explaining to her that she was not in a position to haggle over the prices because there were various other parties involved (caterers and so on) that had to be compensated for their efforts. And that these other parties don't haggle over the fees that they charge the spa owner. It was insane. I knew this woman would have never tried this at a White-owned spa.

For all the above reasons, there are few Black firms with more than three attorneys. The few that do exist tend to get most of their money from government-related contracts that are the result of personal political ties. Government budgets are shrinking, like everything else. Most Black attorneys that I know in the Chicago area who are in private practice are hustling for all the above reasons. They spend most of their time chasing down their clients for their money. Collection issues take up much of their time.

The Black attorneys I know who don't have to hustle are doing better financially because they are hiding behind a White front partner. The White front gets the business, and the Black attorney does the actual work.

Understand and conquer your terrain. It's not the same as it is for non-Black business owners. Don't directly try to attack and overcome customer racism and irrational resistance (including Black customers' anti-Black racism). Don't waste your time lamenting or arguing about the slave mentality that creates this situation for African-American business owners. Gracefully sidestep all of that madness by either having a colorless business, or by being secretive about the fact that your business is Black-owned. Work around this consumer racism and irrational resistance.

- Are you willing to make an honest assessment of your business terrain as a Black business owner?
- Will you avoid wasting time lamenting the slave mentality of African American consumers that says that the White man's ice is colder?
- Will you avoid wasting time lamenting the anti-Black racism of non-Black consumers?
- Are you willing to do what it takes to sidestep all of that madness?
- Are you willing to have a colorless business, or be secretive about the fact that your business is Black-owned?

PART VI: THE SOJOURNER'S PASSPORT TO LIVING YOUR WILDEST DREAMS

CHAPTER 34

BLACK WOMEN NEED NEW DREAMS AND A BLACK WOMEN'S ARTS MOVEMENT

A Prayer for New Visions for African-American Women

Please, Lord, no more art that depicts African-American women as traumatized losers. No more African-American art that plumbs the depths of depravity. Please, Lord, deliver African-American women and girls from any further exposure to this type of material. Guide us to life-giving, spirit-nourishing, victorious material. Guide us to create life-giving, spirit-nourishing material that portrays healthy images of ourselves. Amen.

The Current Art Directed at African-American Women Is Grounded in Masochism

Most art directed at African-American women is grounded in masochism. Let's reflect on this for a moment. Let's consider the sort of entertainment products that African-American women and girls have normalized. We seek out and consume entertainment products that showcase women and girls like ourselves being emotionally abused, beaten, molested, and raped. How did this sort of material become a steady source of entertainment for us?

This is sick.

The Current Art Portrays Trauma and Depravity as Normal Parts of Black Women's Lives

We don't understand that repeatedly showing trauma and de-pravity serves to normalize such things. Even when it's done under the guise of showing somebody supposedly overcoming the de-pravity. This is what's wrong with reality television. Things were better before people started openly broadcasting all the sick and depraved things they did or that were done to them.

Some things do belong underground, in the closet, on the fringes, and not spoken of in polite company.

Whites restrict (and keep on the fringes) such bizarre reflections of themselves. Depictions of Whites engaged in depravity is the stuff of Lifetime Channel movies, and "very special" Afterschool Specials. They don't create and consume a constant stream of such images of themselves.

The norm is not to depict a White family as emotionally, physi-cally, or sexually abusing their children. The norm is not to depict a White teenage girl as pregnant, emotionally abused, beaten, raped, or sexually molested. White artists mostly portray their col-lective as composed of decent, wholesome, and healthy people.

I don't have a problem with dystopian works. I loved Octavia Butler's *Parable of the Sower* and *Parable of The Talents* books. It's not the presence of problems that I take exception to. It's who and what are consistently defined as "the problem."

Most dystopian literature and screenplays define the problem as emanating from the society itself. There can be flawed and even evil characters, but most of the problem stems from some extreme flaw from within the society that is the story's setting. Something has gone horribly wrong with the society in which the characters live. Typically, the problem is the existence of conditions such as police states, catastrophic global warming, prolonged economic crashes, fundamentalism, and science gone astray.

Meanwhile, the current traumatic, demeaning art directed at African-Americans positions them as being the problem—and the source of most, if not all, evil. We're almost never shown to be normal, healthy people. Instead, there is a constant stream of entertainment products that portray African-Americans as problems to be dealt with.

Other people are much more careful with their image. Other people are more aware of how their images serve to position them in the global village. For example, note how Jewish people present and portray their Holocaust. Note the difference between this and the way African-Americans play with (and allow other others to play with) the portrayal of slavery in this country.

Also note how, even if the White character dies at the end of the story, White artists still have that story end on a high note. For example, think of the last image in the movie *Thelma and Louise*. The audience does not get to see them broken and dead. Instead, the audience's last glimpse of these characters is of them choosing their own fate.

We need to understand that what looks like compassion isn't necessarily so. Sometimes what looks like compassion is a clever way of stigmatizing us. These stigmatizing images of ourselves that we've bought into hinder our collective ability to escape into healthier environments.

The Current Art Stigmatizes African-American Women

I realize that artists are often working through their own issues in their art. The problem is that Black female artists' public forms of catharsis are damaging to our collective interests. The "We Are Dysfunction" banner that Black female artists have been waving for the past few decades has tightened into a noose around our necks. This noose gets tighter with each new and increasingly repellent image of ourselves that gets beamed around the planet.

The stigmata that we attach to ourselves are hindering our escape into healthier environments and connections with healthier people.

Black female artists' public showcasing of their wounds serves to keep other Black women trapped in the damaging environments that inflicted the wounds in the first place. We can't afford any more of their public catharsis. Their showcasing of their wounds needs to be pushed back into the fringes.

Many of us empathize with Black female victim-artists, but not at the expense of our collective future. Not at the expense of unintentionally narrowing our daughters' options. What was done to these Black female victim-artists is already done. There's no undoing it. The best we can do is prevent the creation of new victims. The way to do this is to keep the escape routes open for other Black women and girls. This means rejecting all images that stigmatize them. Regrettably, this also means that we'll probably have to shove these Black female victim-artists out of the way. Unfortunately, their actions serve to block the escape routes.

We have to out-shout and out-promote our new, positive, attractive "brand" over that of destructive Black female victim-artists. I am sorry that it has come to this. But this is for our collective future. This is for our daughters' futures. This is for keeps.

Modern African-American Artists are Complicit in Oppression

African-Americans generally don't look at anything with a critical eye. Whether it's art, politics, or anything else. Whatever it is, we swallow it down whole without any scrutiny of what we're taking in. This is why those African-American artists who claim to care about African-American people need to be careful about what they present to us. They have to be mindful there are entities out there (basically the entire entertainment industrial complex in its current form) that want to promote only destructive ideas to African-American consumers.

Modern African-American Artists are Destroying Our Cultural Heritage

The entertainment industry's drive to promote poisonous ideas to Blacks is why I refuse to give Sister Souljah a pass about the damage that her work has done to African-American literature. She has much to answer for in popularizing the trash that calls itself "street literature." Because of her pioneering work in this genre, degrading street-literature garbage has almost totally replaced legitimate African-American fiction on bookstore shelves.

This is similar to the stagnation of African-American music after the arrival of the hip-hop poison. At the beginning of hip-hop, most African-Americans had the common sense to realize that what these rappers were doing was inferior. So, we made excuses for their lack of talent. "They're too poor to take lessons; they're too poor to buy instruments; they have to express their 'creativity' in other ways…"

As time went on, no-talent hip-hop products (screaming and cursing over recycled beats from other people's compositions) became normalized as "music" to us. Then African-Americans began defending and justifying hip-hop trash as if it were synonymous with Blackness. I watched over the years as African-Americans who knew better (myself included at one point) were intimidated into silence about the inferiority of rap and hip-hop.

I was a teenager at the start of the rap garbage. Many Black teenagers at the time hated rap. I remember my boyfriend and his male friends grumbling, *"This stuff they're chanting about is messed up, and people are shaking their rumps to this?"* My female friends and I were also grumbling. Unfortunately, we allowed ourselves to be silenced by accusations that we were being "bourgie" (which, of course, is a bad thing—having the life circumstances that our grandparents prayed we would have is a bad thing) when we expressed our dislike of rap and hip-hop.

Then it became almost forbidden to point out the lack of talent or skill involved in creating hip-hop and rap. It was also forbidden to point out how demeaning, degrading, and increasingly destructive hip-hop and rap products were becoming. Hip-hop's many defenders screamed that African-Americans should not mobilize to stop the spread of various destructive hip-hop products. These same defenders screamed that we should support "positive" hip-hop artists *instead of* refusing to support the destructive artists.

Most African-Americans bought into these sorts of arguments. We can all see the results of following this strategy. It failed. Miserably. Our people are so much worse off for it. Because Blacks followed the *"instead of stopping degrading Entertainer X, we should do Y"* strategy, the degrading images and music that some of us want removed are now a thousand times worse than before, and even more widespread.

Buying into these arguments was a huge mistake. If you don't remove weeds, they will eventually crowd out and replace whatever flowers you plant. Unopposed negativity will take center stage, and pave the way for even worse forms of negativity. This has been our experience with hip-hop. **This is because unopposed aggression always escalates and expands its range.** These self-hating and Black woman-hating entertainment products are acts of aggression.

If African-Americans had stopped some of these earlier rappers, we wouldn't be dealing with the filth that we're dealing with right now.

As more time passed, hip-hop garbage became all that most of us know. Our defense of garbage is why most modern African-American music "artists" don't have any basic music skills. They can't read music, play instruments, or sing. Ultimately, our defense of garbage is the underlying reason African-American music has stagnated for the past twenty-five years. African-Americans used to come up with a new style of music every decade or so. Not anymore. Not since the hip-hop trash spread unchecked. Our entertainers went from being people who could sing a cappella on street corners to no-singing, no-instrument-playing hacks who steal beats and melodies from twenty-five years ago.

A similar destructive process is happening with African-American literature. People are now raising the same failed arguments in support of street literature. The identical excuses that were made at the beginning of rap are now being made for no-talent writers. Unless we push back right now, street literature will come to define African-American literature in the future.

This is a travesty that was unnecessary. There were other paths open to Sister Souljah. She didn't have to promote the lowest common denominator in her fiction directed to Black consumers.

I recently read the book *Always Wear Joy* by Susan Fales-Hill. It was about her mother, entertainer Josephine Premice. The book detailed several examples of how Black female artists in previous generations were often robbed of any meaningful opportunities to practice their craft. This history is what makes modern Black female artists' passivity all the more outrageous. Ms. Premice, Diahann Carrol, and others did not have any of the modern tools to leap-frog over the industry gatekeepers and offer their art directly to an audience. They didn't have tools like viral marketing, YouTube, or print-on-demand publishing. They were trapped in having to beg others (such as racist Whites and Black male promoters who hated Black women) for a chance to practice their art.

I've noticed that several White female artists have made more sensible moves. I've noticed that several White actresses who don't even need to do so formed their own production companies. Jodie Foster (who has been in a position to do whatever she wants to do for some time) and Jennifer Aniston are examples of White actresses who did this.

I was pleased to read that Angela Bassett and her husband Courtney Vance formed their own production company. But I wonder why it took so long for Ms. Bassett to wake up and do this. She's at least fifty years old. She looks great, at least a decade younger than her age. But the harsh reality is that she squandered most of her prime acting years waiting for somebody else to offer her roles—instead of creating her own opportunities with her own production company.

Age-discrimination against women artists is wrong, but it's reality. Ms. Bassett should have started her production company at least fifteen years ago. I'm curious to see if Nia Long or Sanaa Lathan wake up before it's too late. The career clock is ticking on them and other African-American actresses in their thirties.

African-American artists need to let go of the addictive fantasy of having stardom handed to them on a platter the same way it is for White artists. For example, I'm constantly amazed at how White Hollywood makes room for, and elevates, foreign White actors. Let's just consider some from one country: Australia. Russell Crowe, Hugh Jackman, Heath Ledger, Eric Bana, Cate Blanchett, Nicole Kidman, and Naomi Watts are examples of foreign White actors who have been elevated by White Hollywood. Hollywood won't do the same thing for Black performers.

African-American actresses need to understand that there's a narrow window of opportunity for them to practice their craft. It's similar to women's narrow window of opportunity for childbearing. Since nobody is going to hand stardom to Black actresses on a platter, they need to hit the ground running. They need to look for ways to create their own opportunities, instead of waiting to be cast in somebody else's project.

Black Women Need New Dreams and a New Arts Movement

African-American women need new dreams. We need new art that encourages healthy, new visions for us. We need our minds focused on the possibilities that are already available to us, and on creating new possibilities for ourselves. We need a Black women's arts movement.

Nobody is going to provide these new images and dreams for

us but us. This is why I'm challenging all you aspiring artists to get busy. Right now! We desperately need your work. We need to create a body of work showing all sorts of Black female protagonists accomplishing all sorts of things in all sorts of settings. I'm not talking about producing novels and screenplays that are explicitly political. I'm talking about Black female artists creating a body of work that paints new possibilities for the Black women and girls who consume these works.

We need to create a new cultural inheritance for the Black women and girls who come after us. We need sojourner-artists to replace the current victim-artists. We need a new, sojourner aesthetic to replace the current one of entrapment. The sojourner aesthetic is a broad one. The only criterion is the answer to the following question: *Does this work promote freedom of movement and healthy, fulfilling possibilities for African-American women and girls?*

We need new dreams. We need these new dreams right now. We can't afford to follow our informal tradition of creatively listing all the reasons what we need is impossible. We also can't continue to put our responsibilities off onto the next generation. I'm not talking about encouraging the children to get involved in the arts. We can't wait any longer for a new body of work. While we're waiting, Black female victim-artists are beaming increasingly repellent images of Black women around the globe. Right now, there's next to nothing to counteract the stigmatizing images they are promoting.

I'm challenging all of us who are capable (that would be me, you, and others) to start meeting this need now. Not after we have homes with specially designed "writing rooms." Now. If we are committed, then we will find ways to do what needs to be done. And not wait until it's convenient, comfy, and cozy to do so. Everyone who believes that quality writing can only be done under perfect conditions needs to remember Dr. King's "Letter From A Birmingham Jail."

We need art that shows the possibilities that are available for African-American women and girls to live healthy, fulfilling lives. We need art that encourages African-American women and girls to seize these possibilities. We need new dreams.

CHAPTER 35

HAVE YOUR OWN 'WILDEST DREAMS' TOUR!

Tina Turner's 'Wildest Dreams' Tour

I always liked the cover photo from Tina Turner's *"Wildest Dreams"* album. Unlike the pornographic contortions that can be found on the covers of many female artists' albums, Ms. Turner looks like she's self-possessed and doing her own thing in this picture. I also appreciated the confident tone of the album title.

The *Wildest Dreams Tour* was a record-breaking, worldwide concert tour from May 1, 1996 to August 10, 1997. It sold out stadiums and arenas all over the world. Good for Ms. Turner.

More African-American women need to embrace and pursue their wildest dreams, instead of what many of us are doing, which is surrendering to a waking nightmare. It's a nightmare of expanding waistlines and receding hairlines.

Expanding Waistlines

Let's get real for a moment. There is a lot of obesity within the African-American community, and it's getting worse with each year that passes. There seem to be many overlapping issues underlying this phenomenon.

Weight gain and college. There seems to be a phenomenon known as "the freshman five" (through fifteen), where many students gain weight during their freshman year. I suspect that freedom from home cooking (combined with much more fast food) has something to do with this.

Weight gain to (psychologically) fend off sexual predators. I've heard this a lot from various Black and Latina women over the years. They've said that being heavier somehow made them feel safer in their communities. Apparently, White women living in White communities do not have to walk a gauntlet of menacing and potentially deadly leers everyday.

I don't know what's going on in Latino communities, but I do know there are serious reasons for Black women to be afraid in Black residential areas. How an African-American woman responds to catcalls and advances from Damaged Beyond Repair Black men (DBRBM) can make the difference between life and death. Increasing numbers of DBRBM are shooting the Black women who refuse their advances.

A DBRBM shot Mildred Beaubrun in May 2008, for refusing his advances. Ms. Beaubrun, who was eighteen years old at the time of the shooting, died the next month. In August 2008, a DBRBM shot Vernice Morris twice after she refused to give out her phone number. Ms. Morris survived. A DBRBM shot two women who refused his advances in May 2009. He shot one woman in the face and the other in the chest. They survived. ("Rejected man shot two women, police say," The Atlanta Journal Constitution, May 21, 2009).

It's understandable that some Black women remain overweight in a misguided attempt to feel safe from DBRBM's potentially lethal street harassment. The final tragedy is that the sexual predators win in the end when women do this. The sexual predators ultimately win because women who do this are unwittingly digging their own graves with their forks.

Other patterns of Black obesity. Some of it might be regional. I've noticed that random Black folks in Chicago are bigger overall than random Black folks I've seen in Manhattan. I suspect that this is due to Manhattan being a walking sort of place. So, the everyday lifestyle is naturally less sedentary. Perhaps it's also due to the higher percentage of immigrants. I haven't spent enough time in the South to notice any patterns there.

I've noticed that Black "church ladies" tend to be bigger than the non-churched. Most of the Black hijab-wearing Muslimahs that I've seen tend to be overweight or obese. Scariest of all, I've noticed that Black children are heavier than they've ever been before. Increasing numbers of African-American children are also suffering from the health complications that result from obesity.

Receding Hairlines

I've also noted the trend that increasing numbers of Black women have hair that looks obviously damaged. I've heard Black hairstylists talking about this. Many of them have noticed it too. There were always the problems caused by long-term mistreatment of one's hair. There were always those women who suffered burns, breakage, and temporary hair loss due to extremely harsh perms.

There were always the problems caused by a long-term habit of wearing too-tightly braided styles (for example, Susan Taylor's braids), severe ponytails, and lacquered and gelled hair. These problems traditionally took years to manifest in permanent damage. I've heard a hairstylist comment that she's seeing more Black teenage girls and women in their twenties with the hair problems that she previously only saw in large numbers with Black women in their forties and older.

For Many Black Women, Stress Is Killing Them Softly

Stress kills. For many African-American women, stress is killing them softly. The stress caused by the various forms of hatred inflicted on Black women has a lot to do with the expanding waistlines and receding hairlines. When I was in high school, I watched how the hair on the back of my best friend's head would break off and fall out whenever there was drama between her parents. One of my Latina colleagues told me about how her eyebrows started to come out when she transferred from working in a misdemeanor courtroom to a major felony courtroom. The damage caused by the emotional, verbal, and physical attacks that Black women are subjected to is no joke.

The Resistance to Self-Elevation

It seems to me that many African-American women have grown so weary from fending off attacks to our dignity, that we defensively support mediocrity, surrender, and failure in all forms. Many of us have a knee-jerk reflex of defending whatever is subpar.

"I can be big and beautiful!" Perhaps, but you're also not at your very best.

"I'm good enough just as I am. Not everybody wants to reach for excellence. I don't want to reach for excellence. I'm just fine the way I am!" Perhaps, but you're also not at your very best.

These responses remind me of Vince Lombardi's observation that once people learn to quit, quitting becomes a habit.

We also sometimes choose to interpret calls for self-elevation and excellence as calls for imitating White dysfunction. I don't want to talk about White women's body image issues. I don't want to talk about the messages that are promoted in White women's magazines. White women were never programmed to believe that they are inferior to every other race of women in terms of beauty. White women are taught that they are the pinnacle of female beauty.

White women's context is not our context. White women were never subjected to beauty standards that eliminate most of them from being considered beautiful. White women's color, features, and hair textures are not subjected to ridicule, disdain, and hatred.

White women's context is not our context. White women have their presumed beauty publicly recognized, ratified, and treasured not just by White men, but by every race of men on this planet. Including legions of self-hating, White-worshipping men of color.

White women's context is not our context. White women aren't dropping like flies from weight-related ailments like high blood pressure and diabetes as African-American women are.

White women's context is not our context. Between White women and us, which category of women is mostly downtrodden, hated, disrespected, self-hating, and self-disrespecting? Between White women and us, who is in more need of lifting the value we place on ourselves?

White women already have the dominant spot carved out for them on the global stage. Meanwhile, Black women have been shoved off this stage for centuries. We've had our rightful place stolen from us. We've been programmed to be satisfied with watching from the back rows.

It is fitting and appropriate for Black women to take the necessary steps to regain our rightful place. Part of this process has to do with our self-presentation. More of us need and deserve the benefits that accrue from stepping up our game. Please don't try to twist this around into a discussion of how we must avoid White women's dysfunctions. That is not our problem. White women's problems are not the problems that we are facing.

We Can Fight Back By Pursuing Our Wildest Dreams

We can fight back against the onslaught of soul-damaging, life-damaging attacks. We can do this by embracing and pursuing our wildest dreams. We don't need anybody's permission to stage our own Wildest Dreams Tours. It's best to start with the things that are under our direct control. Like how we treat our own bodies.

We don't have to accept a waking nightmare of expanding waistlines and receding hairlines. We can get our college-aged bodies back if we are willing to do the work. Those of us who didn't have bodies that we were pleased with in college, can work to have them now. We can improve our nutrition to help our hair. We can strive to remove ourselves from negative, stress-inducing surroundings. We can start with baby steps.

- Are you committed to treating yourself better?
- Are you committed to starting with the things that are under your direct control?
- Are you committed to treating your body better?
- Are you committed to pursuing your wildest dreams?

CHAPTER **36**

WILDEST DREAMS CHECKLIST: WILL YOU BE READY FOR YOUR BREAKTHROUGH MOMENT WHEN IT ARRIVES?

Potential breakthrough moments happen more often than we realize. The problem is that most people aren't prepared to take advantage of them when they happen. This is how people miss opportunities.

A reader brought Natalie White to my attention. Ms. White is a sister who's busy becoming a pop star in South Korea. It seems that South Koreans started watching the YouTube videos that Ms. White (who goes by the name "Pumashock") posted of herself performing R&B-influenced renditions of Korean pop songs. This led to a mini-craze, which led to being invited to South Korea to appear on the television show *Star King*. All of which has led to contacts within the South Korean entertainment industry. Ms. White has been in the news, including one news story featured on the South Korean government's official Web site. You can see it here: http://www.korea.net/news/news/newsView. asp?serial_no=20090311001

I found a couple of things interesting about all of this. First,

Ms. White is not of Korean ancestry. This seems to be an example of a non-exotic, "typical," Black woman exercising her right to live as a global citizen—and finding success on the global stage. More power to her.

Second, I don't believe for a moment that she decided *on a whim* to post her performance videos on YouTube. It's obvious from the professional quality of her videos that she prepared for her breakthrough moment. In fact, she might have already had an agent or manager who helped make it happen by designing a YouTube marketing strategy for her.

Ms. White was obviously ready when her breakthrough moment came. Are you ready for your breakthrough moment?

- Are your skills polished?
- Are you flawless in terms of your outer presentation?
- In other words, are you ready for prime time right now? If not, are you getting yourself ready?
- Are you ready to handle the envy and resentment that is sure to come once you make your breakthrough?

CHAPTER 37

WILDEST DREAMS CHECKLIST: REBOOT YOUR LIFE BY BECOMING 'UNREASONABLE'

My car is nearing the end of its service life. It's a Hyundai. I like it, and it has served me well over the past nine years. However, I can see that it's almost time for me to move on and get another car. Since I don't like long-term debt, I've been saving so I can pay for at least 90 percent of the next car upfront (which is what I did when I bought the Hyundai).

So, what will I buy? I can be reasonable in one sense and buy another new Hyundai. Or I can be unreasonable, and spend roughly the same amount of money on a used BMW. I'm leaning toward the BMW.

This isn't about name brands (although I must admit that I *like* the idea of giving my former supervisor, and the few other workplace haters yet another reason to be annoyed with me). I've never cared about brands, and I was happy to choose my Hyundai. It's about pleasure and amusement. Mine. A friend's daughter has a BMW, and I've thoroughly enjoyed riding in it. I deserve to have *whatever* I want.

This also is not about being reckless. If we look hard enough, we can find lower-risk ways of enjoying what we want. Doing so takes determination and creativity.

I was reminded of all of this by a reader's questions recently. The discussion was about Black women's divestment from all non-reciprocating entities (Black residential areas, most Black organizations, non-reciprocating Black men). Instead of looking for ways to make divestment work, the reader was creative in coming up with implausible and downright peculiar imagined obstacles to Black women's divestment. This was despite the numerous living examples of Black men who have divested from the African-American collective over the decades.

It was strange. I believe that part of it was bad-faith, troll behavior. But it was also an exaggerated version of what so many African-Americans habitually do. We're quick to give up on readily attainable dreams, while simultaneously dropping everything to chase mostly unattainable dreams (such as becoming a professional athlete or rapper).

Compromising with, and ultimately giving up on, one's inner dreams are an unfortunate side effect of becoming a responsible adult. This is why most people live for the weekends. Most working people use weekends and too-rare vacations as a chance to recapture as much missed pleasure as possible. Meanwhile, their daily lives are filled with drudgery. For years. These years turn into decades. These decades turn into an entire lifetime filled with silent resentment about missed opportunities. And that's for people who are blessed to have jobs.

There has to be a better way. There is a better way, if we have the will to look and work for it. Nobody is going to do this for us. Please read and reflect on the following blog post from author Tim Ferriss.

http://www.fourhourworkweek.com/blog/lifestyle-costing/

- Are you willing to become unreasonable?
- Are you willing to find nonreckless ways of having what you want?
- Are you willing to find nonreckless ways of becoming what you want?
- Are you willing to find nonreckless ways of experiencing what you want?

CHAPTER 38

WILDEST DREAMS CHECKLIST: ARE YOU LIVING FOR THE WEEKENDS AND DEAD FOR THE REST OF THE WEEK?

Most people are animated corpses for most of their waking hours. This matches the hours in the day people spend working at jobs that have no connection whatsoever to their values. A while ago, I decided to stop being among the dead.

Does Your Current Work Have Any Connection to Your Values?

After I decided to escape into a lifestyle of living during most of the week, I started the practice of using vacation time to give myself frequent three-day weekends. I'm happy I started doing that. I've been using the extra day off from the cemetery as dress rehearsals for what my weekdays will be like once I complete the transition into being self-employed. Yesterday morning was a delightful example of that. Leisurely waking up whenever I wake up; then my morning workout; then a good breakfast; then work on my business stuff. At my own pace, and on my own schedule. I'm loving it!

Do You Understand that the Era of Dependable, 'Good Jobs' Is Over?

It's interesting how tightly people often cling to what is familiar, even when it's unpleasant. It's understandable, especially in terms of making a living. Every normal person who has to work for a living has the same basic fears and financial obligations. That's not a joke, or anything to take lightly.

However, circumstances have changed. Under current conditions, it's dangerous to depend on a single job. The least that people need to do in these current economic circumstances is to develop additional, side income streams.

Wouldn't It Be Nice to Be Alive During the Week, Instead of Counting the Days until the Weekend?

Most working people use weekends and too-rare vacations as a chance to recapture as much missed pleasure as possible. Meanwhile, their daily lives are filled with drudgery. For years. These years turn into decades. These decades turn into an entire lifetime filled with silent resentment about missed opportunities. And that's for people who are blessed to have jobs.

There has to be a better way. There *is* a better way, if we have the will to look and work for it. Nobody is going to do this for us.

This is not about being reckless. If we look hard enough, we can find lower- and medium-risk ways of having the lives that we want. However, doing so takes determination, creativity, and often patience. There is no free lunch.

Most African-Americans have a bad mental habit of learned helplessness. Instead of looking for ways to make our wildest dreams come true, we're creative in coming up with implausible (and downright peculiar) imagined obstacles to having anything that resembles freedom.

I've watched other African-Americans (often angrily) speak

helplessness no matter what is being discussed. I've listened to African-American women wail, *"Where can we go?"* when divestment is under discussion. Somehow it doesn't occur to them that we can go to the same areas that Black men go with their non-Black girlfriends and wives.

I've watched African-Americans whimper, *"How can we get out of poverty?"* Somehow they don't notice the non-English-speaking Mexican men who have created employment for themselves by mowing Black folks' lawns. Nobody prevented African-Americans from making money by cutting grass. Two objects can't occupy the same space at the same time. Mexican men were able to build entire lawn service businesses cutting grass in Black residential areas because Black men *weren't* offering this service. Nature abhors a vacuum. Something will always rush in to fill one.

There are everyday examples of various people stepping over and around African-Americans to accomplish all sorts of goals, and yet we angrily insist that what these other people are doing is impossible. We say this while we are watching them do it.

I know that some (most?) of you are assuming that being alive for most of the week is not possible for you. *Before you limit your possibilities based on untested assumptions,* at least take the time to read the following feature story about a married Black couple who are using lifestyle design ideas to run a micro-multinational company out of their home!

http://www.fourhourworkweek.com/blog/2008/07/08/ mom-and-pop-multinationals-how-to-go-global-plus-call-with-me-and-david-allen-at-12pm-pt/

Also, if you're serious about finding a way to be alive during most of the week, read Tim Ferriss' book, *The 4-Hour Workweek.*

- Wouldn't it be nice to walk away from a dead-end job whose only true purpose is to sustain a deathstyle?

- Wouldn't it be nice to be alive during most of the week, instead of counting the days until the weekend?
- Are you willing to find and work toward nonreckless ways of making this happen?

EPILOGUE

CHAPTER 39

EPILOGUE: A YEAR FROM NOW

Imagine It's a Year from Today

Imagine that it's a year from today, and you're having dinner out with a group of your girlfriends.

They're all in a somewhat sour mood, for one reason or another. One friend is worried about losing her job, and how she'll put food on the table as a single parent. Another friend is stressed out by a job that she can't afford to quit, even though her husband works. She's also exhausted by the constant demands that her relatives make on her time and energy. She's constantly doing favors for them, but they don't extend themselves for her. A third friend is nervous because she doesn't know how her husband will react when she gets home. Her husband constantly switches back and forth from charm to anger to relentless criticism of her, and she's always "walking on eggshells" trying to please him.

You listen with great sympathy, but you're not quite sure what to say.

Inside, you feel blessed and thankful.

You feel blessed and thankful because your situation is totally different from theirs.

A year ago, you started developing additional side-income streams so you don't have to depend on your job. It feels good knowing that you're not completely financially dependent on your employer.

A year ago, you decided to work toward walking away from your unfulfilling job altogether, and into another field where your talents will be appreciated. You're not there yet, but you can see that you're getting closer to achieving this goal.

A year ago, you decided to require reciprocity in all your relationships. Yes, some friends and relatives have distanced themselves from you as a result. But you're much more relaxed than you were before you made this decision. You're relaxed because the current people in your life give as much to you as you give to them. You're being supported and energized by the people around you, instead of being drained.

While all of this is happening, you are also having much more fun in your social life. You're having fun because you stopped restricting yourself to all-Black social circles. You also stopped restricting yourself to the activities that are considered stereotypically Black. You stepped outside your cramped, suffocating, false-comfort zone to take part in all the previously unexplored activities that you've always been curious about.

Along the way, you've been meeting and dating several fascinating, quality men from the global village. Men who share a common interest in your newfound hobbies and activities. Men you never would have met if you had continued to socialize in exclusively Black social circles. Men who appreciate your beauty, intelligence, and high spirits. One man has expressed his interest in a courtship that could lead to marriage.

Life is good, and getting even better.

You Can Make This Come True

The lifestyle described above is not a fairy tale. You can make it come true. You can have a life that you love—when you find the power to love yourself.

Please Accept a Free Gift as My Way of Saying Thanks

As my way of saying thanks for buying this book, please accept a free digital excerpt from my next book, *Daily Meditations For Sojourners*. Please visit www.sojournerspassport.com to download your free excerpt, and stay in touch with other offers and information. All I ask is a small favor in return. If you would like to support this message of empowerment and abundance for Black women, please leave a short customer's review of this book at Amazon.com. Please also tell your friends and family about this book, and maybe give them a polite nudge to get them to buy. Thank you for your support!

CPSIA information can be obtained
at www.ICGtesting.com
Printed in the USA
LVHW031041200322
713908LV00003B/362